The TopFive Guide to
FIGHTING EVILDOERS

---

by Chris White

and the writers of TopFive.com

Copyright © 1994-2002 Chris White and TopFive.com

Published by TopFive Publications.

All right reserved. This book or portions thereof may not be copied or reproduced in any medium without prior written permission from the author.

TopFive Publications
5482 Wilshire Blvd.
Suite 137
Los Angeles, CA 90036

ISBN: 0-9729429-0-4

9 8 7 6 5 4 3 2 1

Cover design by Jeff Scherer

Cover photo copyright © 1999-2003 Getty Images, Inc.
Used with permission.

Printed and bound in the U.S.A.

Serving suggestion: Enjoy with a piping hot beverage on a chilly winter night. Bearskin rug and inflatable partner optional.

Acknowledgments

I would like to thank two friends whose efforts proved invaluable in the creation of this book:

> Jeff Scherer
> cover design, art direction, proofreading

> Peg Warner
> proofreading

Also, thanks to those whose contributions directly led to the Internet success of The Top 5 List and TopFive.com, including:

> Jeffrey Anbinder, Peter Bauer, Geoff Brown, Jonathan Colan, Tristan Fabriani, Fran Fruit, Larry Hollister, Sandra Hull, Doug Johnson, Wade Kwon, Jim Louderback, Kim Moser, Bill Muse, Jim Rosenberg, Lev L. Spiro and Cathie Walker

Very special thanks to:

> Gloria Monti, the eternal rookie

Of course, sincere gratitude and a canned ham go to David Letterman and the *Late Night with David Letterman* writers for giving birth to the "Top 10 List" concept.

Last, but certainly not least: Thanks to the more than 500 individual contributing authors of The Top 5 List, whose consistently inspired and frequently brilliant comedic thoughts make my work an ongoing orgy of mirth and merriment. Woo-hoo, indeed!

Chris White

**Fondly dedicated to
the memory of Don Swain**

The TopFive Guide to
FIGHTING EVILDOERS

Hello, friends and neighbors. As I am a man bearing the greatest of responsibilities, I won't beat around the bush. I wish to speak to you about a serious subject — one that demands alert thinking and quick, decisive action. The side of Good needs your support like it never has before. We are, I'm afraid to say, in the midst of a dark nightmare: Our very way of life is being threatened by an invasion of evildoers!

That's right: evildoers. I say this not to frighten you, but rather to call to your attention an ongoing plot designed to culminate in nothing less than the complete subversion of the American family. Then again... I take it back: You *should* be scared.

Evildoers are everywhere these days. You will not easily spot them, as they wear no uniform, nor do they have nametags. High-powered binoculars are of no use, either. No, you must instead use your guile and your wits, for these heartless barbarians are as clever as they are treacherous. You see, they hide among us, disguised as us. They dine with us, shop in our boutiques, purchase cold cuts at our butcher shops, attend services at our places of worship, sit amidst our children in their classrooms, work inconspicuously in our factories... perhaps even share our beds. There is no limit to the deceit and subterfuge of which these monsters are capable.

They will seduce you with promises of futuristic dream cars, all glistening chrome and capable of flight. They will dangle in front of you the "kitchen of tomorrow," with an array of aluminum appliances designed to make your life easy. They will undoubtedly entice your children with sweet treats in an attempt to lure the little ones to their evil lairs. And they will not rest until they have attained their goal of completely and totally infecting our society. That is why you must act boldly and swiftly to help stamp out this nefarious menace.

At this point, your brain is probably filled with questions. What can a typical American family man do to protect his vulnerable wife and helpless children in the face of such a peril? How can the average Joe combat a threat of this magnitude? That is where this book comes in, my friend, as *The TopFive Guide to Fighting Evildoers* contains simple, yet proven-effective advice for staving off these miscreants.

Here then, are the four steps one should follow to repel this most pernicious of plagues:

1. Learn to recognize the enemy. Among the common facades that evildoers present to the world are: camp counselors, radio "disc jockeys," men who eat moist meat products on subways and buses, women who choose to dress provocatively, customer service representatives, tour guides, ill-mannered adolescents and pre-pubescent beauty queens, actors and comedians and others in the entertainment business, those with an excess of coarse body hair, and hot dog vendors. And mimes and clowns — *exercise extreme caution in the presence of mimes and clowns.*

2. Never trust an evildoer. Remember: You can only count on evildoers to be evildoers!

3. Teach your children to duck and cover.

4. Last, but certainly not least, read the lists and quotes you will find in the following pages of this helpful guide. Commit this material to memory. Upon completion, eat the book. While you never know when and where you might be called upon to do battle with the malevolent menace, you can increase your odds of victory by arming yourself with the ammunition of proper preparation.

Thank you for your invaluable assistance in this most urgent of missions.

> J. Willam Monahan
> Regional Director
> Federal Bureau of Suspicious Persons

The Top 15 Signs You've Hired the Wrong Guy to Remodel Your House

15. Suspicious increase in number of 1-900-DRILLBIT calls charged to your line.

14. Uses "The Clapper" to turn power saw on and off.

13. Paints the living room with 15,000 bottles of White-Out.

12. Shows up with nothing but a strategically placed power drill and a butt crack the size of the Grand Canyon.

11. Flaming pentacle and mutilated goats in your basement.

10. Comes to work with a Bob Vila lunchbox, complete with crazy straw for the thermos.

9. Left hand: sledgehammer
   Right hand: Colt 45 Malt Liquor

8. On the day the insulation is to be put down, shows up wearing Pink Panther costume.

7. Mike Wallace from *60 Minutes* drops by with camera crew.

6. While painting: "One for the wall, one for me, one for the wall...."

5. Keeps asking you to "adjust my tool, if y'know what I mean."

4. His see-through teddy shows that he's confused Victorian Style with Victoria's Secret.

3. Insists on spackling with his genitalia instead of with a trowel.

2. Runs out of shingles and starts using bologna slices.

1. Spends hours in your bathroom flushing the toilet and saying, "Well I'll be goldarned!"

The list on the preceding page is from June 29, 1994.
It was compiled from 154 submissions by 47 contributors.

Ed Brooksbank, Sacramento, CA	– 1
Brian Schroer, University City, MO	– 2, 13
Michele Beltran, Lansing, MI	– 3, 15
Don Horton, Sacramento, CA	– 4
Roger P. Ciotti, Kenosha, WI	– 5
Randy Wohl, Ma'ale Adumim, Israel	– 6
Ken Woo, San Diego, CA	– 7
Burt Paulson, Marysville, WA	– 7
Alan Wagner, Bayside, WI	– 8
Sean Erwin, San Diego, CA	– 9
Patrick Kachurek, Ann Arbor, MI	– 10
Aaron Milenski, Oberlin, MD	– 11, 12
Ken Wilson, Kansas City, MO	– 12
Chris Willis, Boston, MA	– 12
Bruce Ansley, Baltimore, MD	– 12
Sam Evans, Charleston, SC	– 12
John Hering, Alexandria, VA	– 14
Chris White, San Diego, CA	– Topic

Talk about a close call! Just before I mailed the invitations to my dinner party, I luckily realized it would involve getting my friends' saliva all over my nice clean forks and spoons.

(Bob Van Voris)

The journey of a thousand miles starts with a trip to the bathroom.

(Tom Sims)

The Top 20 Food Ideas Rejected by McDonald's

20. McGristle
19. Salmon McNella
18. Tom & Roseanne "Together Forever" Value Meal
17. Shirley McLean Burger
16. McMenudo
15. Filet o' Gefilte Fish
14. Way Too Damn Happy Meal
13. Lion King Hairball Happy Meal
12. Them Ain't Nuggets!
11. McKitty Sandwich
10. Boutrous Boutrous Burger
9. Rocky Mountain McOysters
8. McSpleen
7. The Depressed Meal
6. Filet O' Flesh
5. McShrooms
4. Bob Barker's Happy Pants Meal
3. McTonya Club Sandwich
2. Grumpy Meal, Dopey Meal and Sneezy Meal
1. Chicken McBobbitts

The list on the preceding page is from July 7, 1994.
It was compiled from 178 submissions by 43 contributors.

Roger P. Ciotti, Kenosha, WI	– 1, 3, 10
John Hering, Alexandria, VA	– 1, 12
Elliott Schiff, Pittsburgh, PA	– 1, 17
Sharon Yonkers, Clarksville, TN	– 1
Bill Burnett, Lexington, MA	– 1
Aaron Milenski, Oberlin, OH	– 1
Mike Wolf, Bronx, NY	– 2
Greg Sherwin, Palo Alto, CA	– 4
Ken Woo, San Diego, CA	– 5, 9
Brian Schroer, University City, MO	– 6, 9, 13, 20
Dennis Koho, Keizer, OR	– 7
Randy Wohl, Ma'ale Adumim, Israel	– 8
Marshal Perlman, Palm Bay, FL	– 8
Michele Beltran, Lansing, MI	– 8
Lemon Rinaldi, San Francisco, CA	– 10
Kim Moser, New York, NY	– 10
Jim Louderback, San Francisco, CA	– 11
Wade Kwon, Birmingham, AL	– 14
Jeff Johnson, Daly City, CA	– 15, 20
Joseph Funk, San Francisco, CA	– 16
Chris McFarland, Austin, TX	– 18
Boyd Johnson, San Diego, CA	– 19
David Pilkington, Lake Forest, IL	– 20
Chris White, San Diego, CA	– Topic

Six of one, half a dozen of the other...
that's 12, right? I'm just saying,
they seem to be making it twice
as complicated as it needs to be.

(Slick Sharkey)

The Top 18 Signs Your Mechanic Is Losing It

18. That photo of a naked A.J. Foyt on his wall.

17. You catch him in his office making auto noises and "shifting gears," if you know what I mean.

16. Replaces your fan belt with a pair of bikini underwear.

15. Embroidered "Mr. Bad-Ass Wrench" on his shirt.

14. Hose from air pump leads into his coveralls.

13. Keeps asking if you're sure you don't want a "lube job."

12. Still doing work for O.J. and expecting to get paid.

11. Eats Gojo off finger as if it were peanut butter.

10. Giggles uncontrollably whenever anyone says "lug nuts."

9. "Huh huh, he said 'dipstick.' Huh huh, huh huh."

8. Keeps asking you if you've seen that episode of *Gilligan's Island* where they almost get rescued, but Gilligan screws it up in the end.

7. Believes your Hyundai is possessed by the spirit of Kim Il Sung.

6. Replaces diagnostic computer with Magic 8 Ball.

5. Urinates on your tire and says, "Just markin' my turf."

4. Rewires the cruise control to the radio so that the faster the music, the faster your car goes.

3. Owns no wrenches, but complete set of every size monkey.

2. Looks suspiciously like Joe Piscopo. Wait a minute — he *is* Joe Piscopo!

1. Won't stop humming *The Wheels on the Bus Go 'Round and 'Round*.

The list on the preceding page is from July 13, 1994.
It was compiled from 135 submissions by 44 contributors.

Paul E. Schindler Jr., Orinda, CA	– 1
Kris Lawrence, Greensboro, NC	– 2, 8
John Ruscio, Waltham, MA	– 3
David Pilkington, Lake Forest, IL	– 4
Ed Brooksbank, Sacramento, CA	– 5
Joe Desiderio, New York, NY	– 6
Bruce Ansley, Baltimore, MD	– 7
Alkes Price, Philadelphia, PA	– 9
Michele Marie Beltran, Lansing, MI	– 10, 16
Kim Moser, New York, NY	– 10
Bill Burnett, Lexington, MA	– 11
Tony Hill, Minneapolis, MN	– 12
Tim Blankenbaker, Washington, DC	– 13
John Hering, Alexandria, VA	– 13
Mitch Patterson, Melbourne, FL	– 14
Sam Evans, Charleston, SC	– 15
Galen Tatsuo Komatsu, Hawaii	– 17
Bob Wells, Karlsruhe, Germany	– 18
Chris White, San Diego, CA	– Topic

I've got the best of both worlds —
my mom's eyes and my dad's PIN #.

(Jim Rosenberg)

Home Depot: The place where people
who can't program a VCR are encouraged
to install a hot tub by themselves.

(Brad Osberg)

The Top 19 Rejected Breakfast Cereal Ideas

19. Beerios

18. Kevorkian Krispies

17. Honeymoon Nuts

16. Chernobyl Charms

15. Eboli-O's

14. Cap'n Crack

13. Kellogg's Ganja Puffs

12. Lucky Tabs O' Acid

11. Colostomy Crunch

10. Phil Gramm Crackers

9. Fruit & Fabio

8. Look Again — Them Ain't Raisins!

7. Post-Modern Toasties and Rococo Puffs

6. Limbaugh Logs

5. Kellogg's None of Your Goddamn Business

4. Special AK-47

3. UnaBran

2. Nut 'N' Bitch

1. CaCa Puffs

The list on the preceding page is from May 8, 1996.
It was compiled from 123 submissions by 32 contributors.

Yoram Puius, Bronx, NY	– 1
David Spiro, Tucson, AZ	– 2
Glenn Marcus, Washington, DC	– 3
Tim Blankenbaker, Washington, DC	– 4, 8
Perry Friedman, Palo Alto, CA	– 5, 19
Lemon/Rinaldi, San Francisco, CA	– 6
Phil Woodall, Richmond, VA	– 7, 18
Greg Sherwin, Palo Alto, CA	– 8, 11, 14
Michele Beltran, Lansing, MI	– 8, 9
Steve Hurd, San Ramon, CA	– 10, 16
Christopher Troise, New York, NY	– 12
Ed Brooksbank, Sacramento, CA	– 13
Enrico Leoni, Raleigh, NC	– 14
Gail Celio, E. Lansing, MI	– 15
Bruce Ansley, Baltimore, MD	– 15
Chris White, New York, NY	– 17, Topic
Ken Woo, San Diego, CA	– 18
Rob Wells, Paris, France	– 18
Geoff Brown, Farmington Hills, MI	– 18
Michael Wolf, Bronx, NY	– 19

In my wild youth, we would go out to Dead Man's Run
behind Old McGregor's Farm and play chicken.
I was the champ until Fast Sammy Rivers came
to town and stripped me of my title. Although
all of my friends thought the match was
a little unfair since he had a car and all.

(R.M. Weiner)

The Top 18 Signs That
Ronald McDonald Is Growing Up

18. No longer signs paychecks in crayon.

17. That new Mr. Happy Meal.

16. He's got McPubes.

15. Now prefers to be called Ron McDonald.

14. Distinctive odor of bourbon and stale cigars at personal appearances.

13. Two words: sagging buns.

12. Replacing floppy red shoes with floppy black wingtips.

11. Now offering Happy Hour Meals.

10. Traded in clown suit for long trench coat.

9. No longer asks women if they want to see his McNuggets.

8. Instead of size 46 shoe, now takes a size 62.

7. Gin has replaced make-up as his nose-reddener.

6. Hamburglar? Sleeping with the fishes.

5. Finally realizes that Pauly Shore isn't funny.

4. That telltale bottle of Clairol Fire Engine Red #4 in his shower.

3. Seen with Jack-in-the-Box at strip clubs stuffing fries down g-strings.

2. Three kids injured in unfortunate stubble incident.

1. Has a McBeergut.

The list on the preceding page is from May 10, 1996.
It was compiled from 108 submissions by 34 contributors.

Jesse Guidry, New Orleans, LA	– 1
Ken Woo, Encinitas, CA	– 2
Galen Tatsuo Komatsu, Hawaii	– 3
Steve Maybo, Carlsbad, CA	– 4
Kermit Woodall, Richmond, VA	– 5, 18
Christopher Troise, New York, NY	– 6, 11
Sam Evans, Charleston, SC	– 7
Lemon/Rinaldi, San Francisco, CA	– 8
Tim Blankenbaker, Washington, DC	– 9
Elliott Schiff, Pittsburgh, PA	– 10
Paul Schindler, Orinda, CA	– 12
JB Leibovitch, Oakland, CA	– 13
Norman Kenney, San Diego, CA	– 14
Ward Bahner, Kansas City, MO	– 15
David E. Spiro, Tucson, AZ	– 16
Lee Oeth, San Diego, CA	– 16, 17
Bruce Ansley, Baltimore, MD	– Topic

They say you can't pick your family...
but with a little practice, you *can*
pick them off one by one from the top
of a hill at the family reunion.

(Lili Von Schtupp)

If they can put a man on the moon, you
would think they could get a plastic
dinosaur out of your ass without surgery.

(Scotty G.)

The Top 17 Rejected Titles for the Movie *Twister*

17. *Totally Gone With the Wind*

16. *Lift and Separate*

15. *Boys on the Side... of My Barn*

14. *Summer Film So Full of Special Effects We Couldn't Fit in the Plot*

13. *The Weather Channel: The Movie*

12. *Schindler's Twist*

11. *Field of Debris*

10. *Dead Man Flying*

9. *I, Cumulus*

8. *One House Flew Over the Cuckoo's Nest*

7. *The Splintered Bridges of Madison County*

6. *Wizard of Oz II: The Search for Toto*

5. *Killer Genuine Draft*

4. *Four Weddings and a Funnel*

3. *Indiana Jones and the Trailer Park of Doom*

2. *A Funnel Thing Happened on the Way to the Farm*

1. *Roofless in Seattle*

The list on the preceding page is from May 15, 1996.
It was compiled from 84 submissions from 26 contributors.

Yoram Puius, Bronx, NY	– 1
Perry Friedman, Menlo Park, CA	– 2
Mitch Patterson, Melbourne, FL	– 3
Caroline Gennity, Queens, NY	– 4, 9
Bruce Ansley, Baltimore, MD	– 4, 11, 17
Doug Johnson, Santa Cruz, CA	– 5, 17
Marshal Perlman, Minneapolis, MN	– 6
John Hering, Alexandria, VA	– 7, 10, 15, 17
Jeff Johnson, Daly City, CA	– 8
Lee Oeth, San Diego, CA	– 12
Lemon/Rinaldi, San Francisco, CA	– 12
Sean Erwin, San Diego, CA	– 13, 17
Ed Brooksbank, Sacramento, CA	– 14
Jim Louderback, New York, NY	– 16
Paul Schindler, Orinda, CA	– 17
Bill Burnett, Lexington, MA	– 17
Chris White, New York, NY	– Topic

I don't know about you, but if I ever
saw a man sitting on a park bench
with snot running down his nose,
I certainly wouldn't write a song about it.

(Kathleen Oyanadel)

I always thought that all you have to do is
say you'll sell your soul and the devil shows
up in like two seconds to seal the deal.
Turns out now I have to ask my boss for time
off so I can be home from noon to 5 on Thursday.

(Bob Van Voris)

The Top 16 Signs Your Company Is Planning a Layoff

16. CEO frequently overheard mumbling, "Eeny-Meeny-Miney-Moe."

15. Your workday consists of coming in at 10, thinking up Top 5 List entries with 30 of your coworkers, then leaving at 4.

14. Dr. Kevorkian hired as "transition consultant."

13. Windows 95 shutdown screen reads, "It's Now Safe to Start Looking for Work."

12. Company softball team downsized to chess team.

11. Sudden proliferation of teenage geek interns.

10. Your boss keeps asking you when he can "show your cubicle."

9. Company president now driving a Hyundai.

8. Annual company holiday bash moved from Sheraton banquet room to abandoned Fotomat booth.

7. Old Milwaukee is beer of choice at company picnics.

6. Guard at front desk nervously fingers his revolver whenever you pass by.

5. Giant yard sale in front of corporate headquarters.

4. Babes in marketing suddenly start flirting with dorky personnel manager.

3. Employee Discount Days discontinued at Ammo Attic.

2. Company dental plan now consists of pliers and string.

1. President begins weekly meetings with "Good morning, you ignorant bastards."

The list on the preceding page is from May 22, 1996.
It was compiled from 85 submissions by 32 contributors.

Caroline Gennity, Queens, NY	– 1, 4
Sam Evans, Charleston, SC	– 2
Mitch Patterson, Melbourne, FL	– 3
Doug Johnson, Santa Cruz, CA	– 5, Topic
Bruce Ansley, Baltimore, MD	– 6
Alkes Price, Philadelphia, PA	– 7
John Hering, Alexandria, VA	– 8, 15
JB Leibowitz, Oakland, CA	– 9
Lemon/Rinaldi, San Francisco, CA	– 10
Paul Schindler, Orinda, CA	– 11
Gail Celio, East Lansing, MI	– 12
Kim Moser, New York, NY	– 13
David Hyatt, New York, NY	– 14
Glenn Marcus, Washington, DC	– 14
Duncan Carling, San Francisco, CA	– 16

If I were a clown, I'd cut off my thumb,
then perform the old "disappearing thumb" trick
for little kids — showing them my stump and
then screaming and throwing my thumb at them.
Of course, I'd probably only be able to do it
once, because I doubt I'd get my thumb back.
You know how kids like to keep cool stuff.

(Daniel Likind)

Roses left in water in a vase too long really,
really stink. I'm thinking about calling
them something else so they won't smell as bad.

(Travis Ruetenik)

The Top 16 Signs Your Cat May Be Planning to Kill You

16. Seems mighty chummy with the dog all of a sudden.

15. Unexplained calls to F. Lee Bailey's 900 number on your bill.

14. He actually *does* have your tongue.

13. You find a stash of Feline of Fortune magazines behind the couch.

12. Cyanide pawprints all over the house.

11. You wake up to find a bird's head in your bed.

10. As the wind blows over the grassy knoll in downtown Dallas, you get a faint whiff of catnip.

9. Droppings in litter box spell out REDRUM.

8. Catch him with a new Mohawk looking in the mirror saying, "Mew looking at me? Mew looking at me?"

7. Takes attentive notes every time Itchy and Scratchy are on.

6. You find blueprints for a Rube Goldberg device that starts with a mouse chased into a hole and ends with flaming oil dumped on your bed.

5. Has taken a sudden interest in the woodchipper.

4. Instead of dead birds, leaves cartons of Marlboros on your doorstep.

3. Ball of yarn playfully tied into a hangman's noose.

2. You find a piece of paper labeled "MY WIL" which says "LEEV AWL 2 KAT."

1. Now sharpens claws on your car's brake lines.

The list on the preceding page is from May 31, 1996.
It was compiled from 91 submissions by 27 contributors.

Kermit Woodall, Richmond, VA	– 1
Perry Friedman, Menlo Park, CA	– 2
E Huret, Atlanta, GA	– 3, 10
Galen Komatsu, Hawaii	– 3
Dave George, Arlington, VA	– 4
Gayle Ehrenman, New York, NY	– 5, 16
JB Leibovitch, Oakland, CA	– 6, 13
John Hering, Alexandria, VA	– 7
Christopher Troise, New York, NY	– 8, 13
Michelle Beres, Seattle, WA	– 9
Greg Sherwin, San Francisco, CA	– 9
Patrick Kachurek, Ann Arbor, MI	– 11
David Hyatt, New York, NY	– 12
Jeff Johnson, Daly City, CA	– 13
Rick Welshans, Alexandria, VA	– 13
Marshal Perlman, Minneapolis, MN	– 14
Tony Hill, Minneapolis, MN	– 15
Caroline Gennity, Queens, NY	– Topic

Is it just me,
or does "once upon a time"
sound intentionally vague?

(Alisa Meadows)

The other day, while sitting in
a traffic jam, I thought to myself,
"Why does this only happen to me?"

(Chad Rubey)

The Top 16 Signs Your Inner Child Is Unhappy

16. Hasn't touched your inner train set for days.

15. Spends all day sulking in your lower intestine.

14. You've stopped shouting "Wheeeee!" on the elevator at work.

13. Joins an inner gang and goes wilding through your pancreas.

12. You attempt to overdose on a lethal combination of J&B and M&Ms.

11. When you try to hug him, he pulls away and calls you a "pathetic codependent loser."

10. When your boss calls you incompetent, you reply: "I know you are, but what am I?"

9. Has been sulking since you refused to buy that Power Ranger doll.

8. Constantly whacking the holy hell out of the inner puppy you gave him for his birthday.

7. You keep getting thrown out of bars for ordering Lucky Charms and milk.

6. Primal scream portion of "Bert and Erni"'s Anger Management Workshop" has kept you up three nights in a row.

5. Sudden urge to knock your morning cappuccino and bagel onto the floor.

4. You discover you have an inner Madonna carrying your inner child.

3. Says she can't wait until she's 18 so she can "get the hell outta this dump."

2. You keep your therapist at bay with a Lego Uzi until Gummi bear ransom is delivered.

1. Hires an inner lawyer and slaps your ass with a $40–million inner lawsuit.

The list on the preceding page is from June 4, 1996.
It was compiled from 92 submissions by 28 contributors.

Greg Sherwin, San Francisco, CA	– 1
Doug Johnson, Santa Cruz, CA	– 2, 5, Topic
Caroline Gennity, Queens, NY	– 3, 8, 11
Bruce Ansley, Baltimore, MD	– 4
Meredith Ogden, Ithaca, NY	– 6
Jim Louderback, New York, NY	– 7
Kermit Woodall, Richmond, VA	– 9
Gayle Ehrenman, New York, NY	– 10
Lloyd Jacobson, Washington, DC	– 12
Lee Oeth, San Diego, CA	– 13
Chris McKenna, Malibu, CA	– 14
Wade Kwon, Birmingham, AL	– 15
Tom Louderback, Breckenridge, CO	– 16

Sometimes when I drop my pen, I can't
help but wonder if it's really God's
way of saying he wants to see my butt.

(Colleen Tang)

I ran out of Tupperware one day, so I took
my cottage cheese to work tied up in a condom.
I'm not allowed to use the employee refrigerator anymore.

(Rolf Lundgren)

I invented a new percussion instrument today —
the Bubbaphone. It's just a drunken redneck
beating the crap out of a goat with a 2–by–4.

(Chris Lipe)

I wish I were less awkward around
strangers. I never know what to say
when someone asks me who I am and what
the hell I'm doing in their house.

(Andy Ihnatko)

You always hear about people "going ballistic."
Wouldn't it be a much nicer world
if they went orgasmic instead?

(Dave Henry)

I think the best way to insult an illiterate
bully is to write him a nasty letter.

(Paul Paternoster)

I can't wait until my 20th high school reunion!
The girls are going to kill themselves when
they see all the cool new stuff I've got in my room.

(Jim Rosenberg)

I bet the first hockey game was played with
an animal turd used as a primitive puck.
I also bet that someone had invented the
goalie mask by the end of the first period.

(Chris White)

If I were God, I'd be like,
"People, sacrifice me some burgers."

(Scott Griffin)

When I responded to an ad for a free psychic
reading, she told me I was the type of
person who wants something for nothing.
How could she possibly know that?

(Tom Sims)

I cried because I had no shoes.
Then I met a man who had no feet.
Talk about a day–brightener!

(Brian Jones)

The Internet has revolutionized the way we work.
Just a few years ago, I would have wasted weeks at the
office trying to learn Meat Loaf's real first name.

(J. Hutter)

Some look at a glass and say it's half empty,
and some look at it and say it's half full.
Call me a pragmatist, but at this point I'm
pretty much just looking for the waitress.

(Mark Niebuhr)

The Top 17 Indications Your Family May Be Dysfunctional

17. New bill to ban assault weapons specifically mentions your family.

16. Your vacations are planned through AA instead of AAA.

15. Your mother and your preteen sister always fighting over the last beer.

14. In the middle of family reunion, FBI cuts power to ranch.

13. Bikers next door always complaining about the noise.

12. Local police save money by making your house a precinct substation.

11. Brother is writing nostalgic screenplay, *A Menendez Family Christmas*.

10. Your new little sister is named after a famous serial killer.

9. Holidays usually celebrated by sniffing glue and kicking a toaster around the house.

8. Your son informs you he doesn't care to be your cellmate anymore.

7. You have to buy separate Mother's Day cards for each of Mom's personalities.

6. Family discussions usually begin with "Put the gun down."

5. You *finally* get your work published in a major newspaper and your rat-bastard brother sics the feds on you.

4. Instead of saying grace before dinner, father reads a passage from *Penthouse Forum*.

3. Thanksgiving dinner consists of Wild Turkey instead of roast turkey.

2. Didn't make today's Top 5 List? Dad holds ya, Mom beats ya.

1. No more sunny breakfast nook now that kitchen is a methamphetamine lab.

The list on the preceding page is from June 10, 1996.
It was compiled from 108 submissions by 35 contributors.

Duncan Carling, San Francisco, CA	– 1, 4, 9
Dave George, Arlington, VA	– 2
Alkes Price, Philadelphia, PA	– 3
Meredith Ogden, Ithaca, NY	– 5
Eric Huret, Atlanta, GA	– 6, Topic
Rebecca Smith, Dallas, TX	– 7, 11
Tom Louderback, Breckenridge, CO	– 8
David Hyatt, New York, NY	– 10
Paul Lara, Temple, TX	– 12
Randy Wohl, Ma'ale Adumim, Israel	– 13
John Hering, Alexandria, VA	– 14
Chris McKenna, Malibu, CA	– 15
Perry Friedman, Menlo Park, CA	– 16
Gerard McDonald, New York, NY	– 17

I recently tried my new passive method of cleaning
my mouth: Rather than brushing and killing
innocent germs, I kindly asked them to leave.
It didn't work, though, so I stuck my tongue
in the toaster and fried the little bastards.

(Stevie)

Having a plunger permanently stuck
to your head is one thing, but I bet
what really makes you feel dumb is
throwing a hat on and realizing
you'll never be able to reach it again.

(Davejames)

The Top 18 Least Popular Ben & Jerry's Flavors

18. Idi Amint

17. Wavy Biscuits & Gravy

16. Non-Fat Karen Carpenter Krunch

15. Them Ain't Pralines!

14. Bucket o' Blood

13. DingleBarry Manilow

12. Colon Cannon Crunch

11. New York SuperModel Recycled Fudge Chunks

10. Strawberry Spleen

9. Rocky Roadkill

8. Chock Full o' Montana Nuts

7. Urinal Mint Chip

6. Vapo-Rub Menthol Chunk

5. Snoop Fudgy Fudge

4. Spanky Monkey

3. Brad Pittstachio

2. Bury Garcia

1. Michael Jackson Almost Vanilla

The list on the preceding page is from June 13, 1995.
It was compiled from 107 submissions by 31 contributors.

Dennis Koho, Keizer, OR	– 1
Lee Oeth, San Diego, CA	– 2
Ed Brooksbank, Sacramento, CA	– 2
Sterling Smith, Houston, TX	– 3, 5
Sam Evans, Charleston, SC	– 4
Meredith Ogden, Ithaca, NY	– 6
Perry Friedman, Menlo Park, CA	– 7
Matt Alford, Salem, OR	– 8
Geoffrey Marsh, Beltsville, MD	– 9
Gayle Ehrenman, New York, NY	– 10
Lloyd Jacobson, Washington DC	– 11, 18
Mike Manion, Lexington, KY	– 12
Pete Brittingham, Titusville, NJ	– 13
Mitch Patterson, Melbourne, FL	– 14
Michele Beltran, Lansing, MI	– 15
Jay Allen, Santa Barbara, CA	– 16
Doug Johnson, Santa Cruz, CA	– 17
Tim Blankenbaker, Washington, DC	– Topic

"He loves me, he loves me not" may not be
an exact science, but it's the only one I've got.
Too bad I don't have any daisies, though, because
tweezing your legs takes longer than you'd think.

(Pamela Rice Hahn)

My friends tell me that I refuse to
grow up, but I know they're just jealous
because they don't have pajamas with feet.

(Tom Sims)

The Top 20 Cool Things About a Car That Goes Faster Than the Speed of Light

20. Sleep till noon, still get to work by 8 a.m.!

19. Doppler shift makes red traffic lights look green.

18. Breaking laws of physics only a misdemeanor in most states.

17. Never in car long enough to hear an entire Madonna song.

16. Carl Sagan and Stephen Hawking keep bugging you to carpool.

15. No one can see you pick your nose while you drive.

14. Lunch breaks in Paris — circa 1792.

13. L.A. to Vegas in 2 nanoseconds.

12. You can stop worrying about being sucked into a black hole driving home from work.

11. You're so thin while driving it, you can even wear horizontal stripes.

10. That deer in your headlights is actually behind you.

9. Kid from Mentos commercial almost guaranteed to lose a limb if he tries to duck through back seat.

8. Traffic enforcement limited to cops with Ph.D.s in quantum physics.

7. Bugs never see you comin'.

6. You can get to the good hookers before Charlie Sheen.

5. Can make a fortune delivering pizza with the slogan "It's there before you order or it's free!"

4. Car makes it from Hollywood to London fast enough to not arouse suspicions of Elizabeth Hurley.

3. License plate: "Me=mc^2"

2. Cigarette butts don't land in the backseat — they land in last week.

1. Chicks dig it.

The list on the preceding page is from June 17, 1996.
It was compiled from 137 submissions from 53 contributors.

Lev L. Spiro, Los Angeles, CA	– 1, 13
Sterling Smith, Houston, TX	– 1, 20
John Voigt, Chicago, IL	– 2
Wade Kwon, Birmingham, AL	– 3
Scott Woolley, Cambridge MA	– 4, 18
Paul Paternoster, Redwood City, CA	– 5, 19, 20
Steve Hurd, San Ramon, CA	– 5, 8
David Gunter, Auburn, AL	– 5, Topic
David Hyatt, New York, NY	– 6, 15
Jay Allen, Santa Barbara, CA	– 7
Meredith Ogden, Ithaca, NY	– 9
Doug Johnson, Santa Cruz, CA	– 10
Paul Schindler, Orinda, CA	– 11
Mike Manion, Lexington, KY	– 12
Joe Desiderio, New York, NY	– 14
Jennifer Hart, Arlington, VA	– 16
Dave George, Arlington, VA	– 17
Randy Wohl, Ma'ale Adumim, Israel	– 19
Pete Brittingham, Titusville, NJ	– 19
Kermit Woodall, Richmond, VA	– 20

March Madness just hasn't been
the same since John Phillip Sousa died.

(Paul Paternoster)

I'll bet the reason more people don't graduate
from rodeo clown school is because they don't pass
Being Funny While Getting Gored in the Ass 101.

(Chris White)

The Top 20 Least Impressive Mafia Nicknames

20. Vinny "The Cosmetologist" Scandaliotta
19. Leo "The Raging Codependent" Pacioni
18. Alphonse "The Senator" D'Amato
17. Herbie "The Accountant" Schwartz
16. Rocco "The Rotarian" Manera
15. Frankie "Right Turn on Red" Ragusa
14. Warren "The Webmaster" Larotta
13. Floyd "The Barber" Barboni
12. Angelo "Spastic Colon" Gasdrulli
11. Mario "The Italian Scallion" Cipolla
10. Mikey "Rubber Glove" Spinetti
9. Carmine "The Lovely Swan" Carpecci
8. Nick "Paper Cut" Carlucci
7. Bobby "You Wan' Fries Wid Dat?" Minera
6. Enzo "I Didn't Mean Nothing by That" Garelli
5. Jimmy "The Guy Who Scratches His Fingernails on the Chalkboard" Genarro
4. Vito "Shaved Back" Laroo
3. Tony "The Chia Pet" Gravano
2. The Hitman Formerly Known as Vince
1. Vinnie "Say It With Flowers" LaRosa

The list on the preceding page is from June 20, 1996.
It was compiled from 163 submissions by 45 contributors.

Paul Schindler, Orinda, CA	– 1
Wade Kwon, Birmingham, AL	– 2
Marc Cukier, Toronto, Canada	– 2
Tom Louderback, Breckenridge, CO	– 3
Stephen Pace, Houston, TX	– 4
Paul Paternoster, Redwood City, CA	– 5
Caroline Gennity, Virginia Beach, VA	– 6, 18, Topic
Kermit Woodall, Richmond, VA	– 7, 15
Bruce Ansley, Baltimore, MD	– 8
Dave George, Arlington, VA	– 9
Joel McClure, Sterling Heights, MI	– 10
Tim Blankenbaker, Washington, DC	– 11
Mick McLean, Laramie, WY	– 12
Sterling Smith, Houston, TX	– 13
Ken Woo, Encinitas, CA	– 14
Rebecca Smith, Dallas, TX	– 16
Greg Sherwin, San Francisco, CA	– 17
Dennis Koho, Keizer, OR	– 18
Steve Hurd, San Ramon, CA	– 19
Sam Maranto, Baltimore, MD	– 20

I know I must be really good in bed,
because women always ask me if there's any
possible way I could make it last longer.

(Steve McCann)

Sometimes I get to thinking...
but I can usually nip *that* in
the bud by turning on the TV.

(Larry Hollister)

The Top 20 Least Popular Summer Camps

20. Camp Lactose Intolerance

19. Camp Awannagopeepee

18. Camp Colonic

17. Ranger Packwood's Kamp Touchee-Feelee

16. Camp LardAss

15. Father Stephen's Naturalist Altar Boy Camp

14. Camp OS/2

13. Camp Turnyerhedncoff

12. Marvin's Learn-to-Set-the-VCR-Clock Camp

11. Camp Time/Life Books

10. Camp Squeal-Like-a-Pig

9. Lil' Toiler Textile Mill & Summer Camp

8. Camp Ritalin

7. Camp Wutchoolookinat, NYC

6. The M. Jackson Camp for Cute Young Unchaperoned Boys

5. Lyle and Erik's Wilderness Ranch for Mom & Dad

4. Joe Piscopo's Comedy Workout Camp

3. Camp La Cage

2. Hyalooza Computer Camp

1. Bring-Your-Mommy Sissy-Boy Camp

The list on the preceding page is from July 2, 1996. It was compiled from 146 submissions by 58 contributors.

Meredith Ogden, Ithaca, NY	– 1, 8
Dave George, Arlington, VA	– 2
Chuck Smith, Woodbridge, VA	– 3
Joel McClure, Sterling Heights, MI	– 4
Sam Evans, Charleston, SC	– 5
Chris McKenna, Malibu, CA	– 6
Matthew Diamond, Holland, PA	– 6
Pete Brittingham, Titusville, NJ	– 6
Peg Warner, Bangor, ME	– 7
Duncan Carling, San Francisco, CA	– 9
Randy Wohl, Ma'ale Adumim, Israel	– 10
David Sklar, New Haven, CT	– 11
Kris Kettner, Fond du Lac, WI	– 12
Jennifer Hart, Arlington, VA	– 13
Jackie Gavron, New York, NY	– 14, Topic
Norman Kenney, Carlsbad, CA	– 15
Ed Brooksbank, Sacramento, CA	– 16
Marc Cukier, Toronto, Canada	– 17
Lev L. Spiro, Los Angeles, CA	– 18
Paul Paternoster, Redwood City, CA	– 19
Christopher Troise, New York, NY	– 20

Nothing says "That's funny!" like causing Grandma to laugh up a snot bubble.

(Gary R. Smith)

I'm finally living out my lifelong dream of being a farmer. Now if I could just figure out how to milk all these ants, I'd be in business.

(Stephanie Thompson)

The Top 20 Rejected Children's Books

20. *Where in the New York Area is Jimmy Hoffa?*

19. *The Unabomber Pop-Up Manifesto and Coloring Book*

18. *The Frog Formerly Known as Prince*

17. *Alice in WonderBraLand*

16. *The Legend of Three-Card Monte*

15. *40 Whacks: Counting With Lizzie*

14. *The Little Engine That Could, if Only That Damned Gout Would Go Away*

13. *Girls Are From Venus, Boys Are From Cootieland*

12. *Where the Wildings Are*

11. *The Little Big Book of Necrophilia*

10. *The J. Edgar Hoover Dress-Up Book*

9. *Joe Camel and the Magic Cancer Stick*

8. *The Crack House at Pooh Corner*

7. *The Dummy's Guide to Crying*

6. *When Mommy Leaves Daddy, and What You Did to Cause It*

5. *Where's Waldo's Wee-Wee?*

4. *The Dyslexic's Big Anagram Book*

3. *Barney's Bleeding and Nobody Can Help*

2. *Things Rich Kids Have but You Never Will*

1. *Furious George Delivers the Mail*

The list on the preceding page is from July 3, 1996.
It was compiled from 166 submissions by 54 contributors.

Blair Bostick, Alexandria, VA	– 1, Topic
Gerard McDonald, New York, NY	– 2
Greg Bell, San Diego, CA	– 3
Chuck Smith, Woodbridge, VA	– 4
Brad Schreiber, Los Angeles, CA	– 5
Dave George, Arlington, VA	– 6
David Hyatt, New York, NY	– 7, 13
Jennifer Hart, Arlington, VA	– 8
Matthew Diamond, Holland, PA	– 9
Eric Huret, Atlanta, GA	– 10
Gene/Cynthia Markins-Dieden, New Haven, CT	– 11
Chris McKenna, Malibu, CA	– 12, 17
David Sklar, New Haven, CT	– 14
Gayle Ehrenman, New York, NY	– 15
John Voigt, Chicago, IL	– 16
Gail Celio, E. Lansing, MI	– 18
Wade Kwon, Birmingham, AL	– 19
Steve Hurd, San Ramon, CA	– 20

You never see this in travel guides, but if you
just stop at the local police station and tell
them that you're the murderer they're looking for,
you'll get a free bed and a meal. Then the next
morning, you just say, "Hey, cops, the joke's on you!"
They'll laugh and laugh – and you save money!

(Dave Brennan)

I think I've figured out why
slugs don't like Margaritas.

(Barbara Rush)

The Top 20 Rejected Crayon Colors

20. Angry Aryan White

19. NASDAQ Red

18. UnaBrown

17. Justice Thomas Only-Appears-to-Be-Black

16. Bill Clinton Pasty-Thigh-White

15. Liver Spot Brown

14. Roquefort

13. RedRum

12. Michael Jackson Approaching-White

11. Agent Orange

10. Varicose Violet

9. George Hamilton Tan

8. Princess Di No-Longer-Royal Blue

7. Divine Brown

6. Old Yeller

5. Burnt Davidian

4. The Color Formerly Known as "Purple"

3. Ochre Winfrey

2. Cuervo Gold

1. Does This Look Infected?

The list on the preceding page is from July 18, 1996. It was compiled from 160 submissions by 45 contributors.

Chuck Smith, Woodbridge, VA	– 1
Lee Oeth, San Diego, CA	– 2, 11
Wade Kwon, Birmingham, AL	– 3
Chris White, New York, NY	– 3
Jennifer Hart, Arlington, VA	– 4, 7
Bill Burnett, Lexington, MA	– 4
Tony Hill, Minneapolis, MN	– 5, 12, 17
David Bryant, Columbia, MD	– 6
Dennis Koho, Keizer, OR	– 8, 12
Lloyd Jacobson, Washington, DC	– 9
Peg Warner, Bangor, ME	– 10
Jeff Johnson, Daly City, CA	– 11
Matt Diamond, Holland, PA	– 12, Topic
Bruce Ansley, Baltimore, MD	– 12
Erika Fowler, New York, NY	– 12
John Voigt, Chicago, IL	– 12
Greg Pettit, Houston, TX	– 12
Yoram Puius, Bronx, NY	– 12
Gail Celio, E. Lansing, MI	– 13
Doug Johnson, Santa Cruz, CA	– 14
Kim Moser, New York, NY	– 15
Randy Wohl, Ma'ale Adumim, Israel	– 16
Paul Paternoster, Redwood City, CA	– 16
Glenn Marcus, Washington, DC	– 18
Lev L. Spiro, Los Angeles, CA	– 19
Caroline Gennity, Virginia Beach, VA	– 20
Steve Hurd, San Ramon, CA	– 20

Whenever I find myself in a really dangerous moment, I stop and ask myself, "What would Steven Seagal do in a situation like this?" Then I go out and make a really crappy movie.

(Tom Sims)

The Top 20 Reasons Dogs Don't Use Computers

20. Can't stick their heads out of Windows 95.
19. "Fetch" command not available on all platforms.
18. Hard to read the monitor with your head cocked to one side.
17. Too difficult to "mark" every website they visit.
16. Can't help attacking the screen when they hear "You've got mail."
15. Fire hydrant icon simply frustrating.
14. Involuntary tail wagging is dead giveaway they're browsing www.pethouse.com instead of working.
13. Keep bruising noses trying to catch that MPEG Frisbee.
12. Not at all fooled by Chuck Wagon screen saver.
11. Still trying to come up with an emoticon that signifies tail-wagging.
10. Oh, but they *will*... with the introduction of the Microsoft Opposable Thumb.
9. Three words: carpal paw syndrome
8. 'Cause dogs ain't *geeks*! Now, cats, on the other hand....
7. Barking in next cube keeps activating *your* voice-recognition software.
6. SmellU-SmellMe still in beta test.
5. SIT and STAY were hard enough, GREP and AWK are out of the question!
4. Saliva-coated mouse gets mighty difficult to manuever.
3. Annoyed by lack of newsgroup, alt.pictures.master's.leg.
2. Butt-sniffing more direct and less deceiving than online chat rooms.
1. TrO{gO DsA[M,bN HyAqR4tDc TgrOo TgYPmE WeIjTyH P;AzWqS,.

The list on the preceding page is from July 24, 1996.
It was compiled from 140 submissions by 47 contributors.

John Hering, Alexandria, VA	– 1
Sterling Smith, Houston, TX	– 1
Bruce Ansley, Baltimore, MD	– 2, 14
Lloyd Jacobson, Washington, DC	– 3, 11
Rob Winchell, Arlington, MA	– 4, 12
Lisa Stepaniak, Dearborn, MI	– 5, 20
Matt Diamond, Holland, PA	– 6, 17
Lee Oeth, San Diego, CA	– 6, 20
Doug Johnson, Santa Cruz, CA	– 7, 9
Marc Cukier, Toronto, Canada	– 8
Vickie Neilson, Carlsbad, CA	– 9
Boyd Johnson, San Diego, CA	– 9
Kermit Woodall, Richmond, VA	– 9
David Hyatt, New York, NY	– 10
Jim Louderback, New York, NY	– 11
Paul Lara, Temple, TX	– 13
Tony Hill, Minneapolis, MN	– 15
Jennifer Hart, Arlington, VA	– 16
Randy Wohl, Ma'ale Adumim, Israel	– 17, 18
Greg Pettit, Houston, TX	– 17, 20
Steve Hurd, San Ramon, CA	– 17, Topic
Ed Brooksbank, Sacramento, CA	– 17
Chris McKenna, Malibu, CA	– 17
Dennis Koho, Keizer, OR	– 19

You can get farther with a kind word and
a gun than you can with just a kind word.
But if you've got the gun and the kind
word *and* you've got a big tray of nice,
crisp bacon to pass around, man, you
can pretty much write your own ticket.

(Andy Ihnatko)

The Top 19 Signs You've Gone to the Wrong Tattoo Parlor

19. Only does patterns by Laura Ashley.

18. While working on your back, the artist keeps mumbling, "Damn... you breathed again."

17. On Sundays they feature their "Number of the Beast" special.

16. Needles sterilized with a quick dip in a shot of Cuervo.

15. Recently had its grant revoked by the NEA.

14. Doesn't offer option between "young Elvis" and "Vegas Elvis."

13. A thousand head of cattle in the waiting room.

12. Artist keeps knocking back slugs from the bottle of rubbing alcohol "just to steady the ol' nerves."

11. Work samples on the walls are actual pieces of skin.

10. "Whaddaya mean you *don't* want a swastika?!?"

9. You ask for roses intertwined around a logic diagram of a basic 4-bit integer divide circuit, and they just have *no idea*.

8. Your appointment is always being rescheduled to accomodate some die-hard KISS fan.

7. Mickey Rourke carried out on a stretcher as you arrive.

6. There is an indescribable existential malaise in the air.

5. Tipper Gore in next chair getting her hair done.

4. The only bikes parked outside are Schwinns and Huffys.

3. You're served petit fours and cappuccino while waiting.

2. Nothing sterile in sight, unless you count the employees with their court-ordered vasectomies.

1. Your "Jesus on the Cross" is constantly mistaken for "Gabe Kaplan Playing Golf."

The list on the preceding page is from July 25, 1996.
It was compiled from 131 submissions by 39 contributors.

John Voigt, Chicago, IL	- 1, 19, Topic
Steve Hurd, San Ramon, CA	- 2
Greg Pettit, Houston, TX	- 3, 11
Duncan Carling, San Francisco, CA	- 4
Dee Anne Phillips, Shreveport, LA	- 5
Chuck Smith, Woodbridge, VA	- 6
Alexander Clemens, San Francisco, CA	- 7
Gail Celio, E. Lansing, MI	- 8
Matt Diamond, Holland, PA	- 9
Yoram Puius, Bronx, NY	- 10
Jim Louderback, New York, NY	- 12, 19
Bruce Ansley, Baltimore, MD	- 12
Norman Kenney, Carlsbad, CA	- 12
Lisa Stepaniak, Dearborn, MI	- 13
Doug Johnson, Santa Cruz, CA	- 13
Boyd Johnson, San Diego, CA	- 13
David Hyatt, New York, NY	- 14, 16
Lloyd Jacobson, Washington, DC	- 15
Larry Baum, La Jolla, CA	- 16
Ericka Fowler, New York, NY	- 17

As I sat there petting my dog, it occurred
to me that it was truly a great idea
to put the fur on the *outside* of pets.

(Anna L. Juarez)

Hey, guys, when you're standing at a
urinal next to another guy, it's always
fun to hum the theme from "Dueling Banjos."

(Bob Van Voris)

If I were a recovering sex addict,
I think I would opt for group therapy.

(Pam Pickard)

I realize that brain cells are dying
all the time. I just hope it's not the
ones that remind me to keep breathing.

(Kevin Freels)

When I was a kid, my mom always told me
that I had to eat everything on my plate
because some kid was starving in China.
Now that that Chinese kid and I are grown up,
he must be getting laid twice a day, because
I haven't seen any action in months.

(Vince Grewe)

I'd like to have a dinner party and invite
John Tesh and Charles Manson. Not for their
company, but because I really dislike John Tesh.

(Steve Hurd)

If a UPS guy snaps and starts killing
people, is that considered "going parcel"?

(Jarrod Bridger)

If someone breaks your heart, just punch them in the head. Oh sure, it seems obvious now, but you'd be amazed at how many people don't think of it when it's relevant. Just punch them in the head. And then go get some ice cream.

(R.M. Weiner)

A bully tried to pick a fight
with me in a bar the other night.
My first instinct was to just walk away.
But then I thought a minute and said to
myself, "Dave, your first instinct was
right. Walk away. Run if you must."
Instincts are good like that.

(Dave George)

If Miss Cleo is so great, how come
she couldn't tell I paid for the
reading with a stolen credit card?

(Anna L. Juarez)

People laugh at me when I tell them
that my wife stole Atlantis. But then
I glare at them with my magic eyes
and they stop, 'cause you just don't
dare laugh at a guy with magic eyes.

(Graham Larue)

The Top 15 Good Things About Going to Hell (Part I)

15. None of that annoying check-in procedure like with St. Peter.

14. That Tony Robbins seminar fire walk trick *finally* pays off!

13. Buffet always has plenty of Lucifer's secret-recipe deviled eggs.

12. Due to recent health code changes, vats of boiling brimstone now use low-fat canola oil.

11. Your "Do you smell something burning?" slays 'em, year after year.

10. Plenty of legal help available for filing wrongful-death lawsuit.

9. Newly passed law: Three strikes and you're back in L.A.

8. Satan's confused attempts to torture masochists can be highly entertaining.

7. Inability to ice skate no longer gets in the way of having fun.

6. No need to pack the parka over Bob Dole's election chances.

5. Well, sure, it's hot — but it's a *dry* heat.

4. Free prostate checks and Pap smears administered daily!

3. The surprisingly entertaining *Hitler and Kathie Lee Show*.

2. Prizes awarded for best crank phone calls to God.

1. 52 smmmmmokin' channels of Jim Carrey!

The list on the preceding page is from August 26, 1996.
It was compiled from 134 submissions by 41 contributors.

Ken Woo, Encinitas, CA	– 1, 14
Debbie Lander, Las Vegas, NV	– 2
Chris McKenna, Malibu, CA	– 3, 5
Alexander Clemens, San Francisco, CA	– 4
Greg Sadosuk, Fairfax, VA	– 5, 14
Lee Oeth, San Diego, CA	– 5
George Olson, Colorado Springs, CO	– 5
Sam Evans, Charleston, SC	– 6
Doug Johnson, Santa Cruz, CA	– 6
Paul Schindler, Orinda, CA	– 7
Larry Baum, La Jolla, CA	– 8, 10
Lev L. Spiro, Los Angeles, CA	– 9
Meredith Ogden, Ithaca, NY	– 10
Bruce Ansley, Baltimore, MD	– 10
Steve Hurd, San Ramon, CA	– 10
David W. James, Los Angeles, CA	– 11
Kim Moser, New York, NY	– 12
Jennifer Ritzinger, Seattle, WA	– 13
Greg Pettit, Houston, TX	– 15
Chris White, New York, NY	– Topic

Nothing says "I wasn't going to send you
a Christmas card until I got one from you"
like receiving a Christmas card on January 8th.

(Janis Williams)

Sure, four-leaf clovers are lucky.
Then again, *all* organisms with
freakish extra appendages are lucky.

(Tommy Jack)

The Top 15 Good Things About Going to Hell (Part II)

15. Everywhere you look, there's a smoking section!

14. Perpetual flame means never having to eat a lukewarm french fry.

13. Upon arrival, you realize it's a big step up from Bakersfield.

12. Your little "blue flame" trick now produces spectacular results.

11. Finally get to meet that Rubik guy and tell him what you think of that @#*&%! cube.

10. There's absolutely no chance you'll be living too close to an amusement park.

9. Party-animal Satan throws one helluva weenie roast!

8. Free Microsoft software for everyone (as per agreement made back in early '80s).

7. Finally rid of that pesky little "conscience angel" on your shoulder.

6. Now that you've followed her advice, you just might get that date with Cindy Crawford.

5. Which would you rather jam to: harps and choirs or Hendrix and Morrison?

4. Every Thursday is Karaoke Night, hosted by Dean Martin and Sammy Davis, Jr.

3. Saturday night WWF tag-team bout between Genghis Khan, Vlad the Impaler and Hitler.

2. Everyone gets a length of pipe and a daily crack at Nancy Kerrigan's knee.

1. Fortune to be made on "Welcome, O.J" T-shirts.

The list on the preceding page is from August 27, 1996.
It was compiled from 134 submissions by 41 contributors.

Joe Desiderio, New York, NY	– 1
Caroline Gennity, Virginia Beach, VA	– 2
LeMel Hebert-Williams, San Francisco, CA	– 3, 7
George Olson, Colorado Springs, CO	– 4, 8
Chris McKenna, Malibu, CA	– 5
Paul Paternoster, Redwood City, CA	– 6
Gayle Ehrenman, New York, NY	– 9
Meredith Ogden, Ithaca, NY	– 10
Ed Brooksbank, Sacramento, CA	– 11
David W. James, Los Angeles, CA	– 12
Steve Hurd, San Ramon, CA	– 13
Galen Tatsuo Komatsu, Hawaii	– 14
Rick Welshans, Alexandria, VA	– 15
Chris White, New York, NY	– Topic

Kids in high school can be really mean.
All the kids used to tease me by saying
my mother was a cheap whore that anyone
in town could have for a quarter.
Of course, I didn't let it bother me.
I would just laugh quietly to myself,
knowing they were being over-charged.

(R.M. Weiner)

Yeah, the theater was crowded, and
yeah, there was clearly a fire, but
I sat quietly and watched that movie.
After all, rules are rules.

(Mark Niebuhr)

The Top 16 Signs You Live Too Close to an Amusement Park

16. Your kid's first word is "getchaballoonshere."

15. You can't afford to buy film for your camera unless you drive to the next county.

14. You buy a swingset for your kids and some hoods from Disney pump your garage full of lead as a warning.

13. Merry-go-round riders constantly yanking out your wife's earrings.

12. There's a bearded lady in your back yard, and your mother-in-law is out of town.

11. You paid for your new Lexus with 43,800,000 skee ball tickets.

10. Can't leave your driveway without backing over picketing Southern Baptists.

9. Your house is on the park map as "Crappyland."

8. Crazy kids hand you a buck, then smash your new Volvo with a sledgehammer.

7. Your cat got a hernia carrying home its last mouse kill.

6. Every meal you've had for the past two months has been served on a stick.

5. Neighborhood hookers require an E ticket.

4. Scooby and his pesky friends search your house for evidence regarding the creepy amusement park owner.

3. The name of the damned place is "Six Flags Over Ed Smith."

2. Your "It's a Small World" insanity plea successfully beats the mass-murder rap.

1. Despite your most amorous pleas, wife demands hand-stamp before re-entry.

The list on the preceding page is from August 28, 1996.
It was compiled from 1,348 submissions by 1,348 subscribers.

Kathleen Buchanan, Tuscaloosa, AL	– 1
Don Dillon, Santa Rosa, CA	– 2
Colin Gray, Dumfries, Scotland	– 2
Patrick Golden, whereabouts unknown	– 2
Ed Smith, Chattanooga, TN	– 3
Theresa Noonan, Highland Park, IL	– 4
Ellen S., whereabouts unknown	– 5
Robert Ostling, Santa Rosa, CA	– 6
Bruce White, Hugo, MN	– 6
Paul Berry, Lake Havasu City, AZ	– 7
Paul Piciocchi, Orlando, FL	– 8
Craig Moe, Chapel Hill, NC	– 9
Dan Angelo, San Bernardino, CA	– 9
Greg O'Neill, Durham, NC	– 9
Don Miller, Marysville, WA	– 10
Elissa Laitin, Newton, MA	– 11
Rick Borchert, Manitoba, Canada	– 12
Jill Rosenberg, New York, NY	– 12
S. Marcantonio, whereabouts unknown	– 13
Carrie, Manitoba, Canada	– 14
Rich Nicholas, Oxnard, CA	– 15
Marttinen Terhi, whereabouts unknown	– 16
Chris White, New York, NY	– Topic

I've decided to dedicate my body to a medical
school, and just before I die, I'm going
to swallow a little plastic toy. That way,
the medical student who cuts me open will
get a nice surprise. I just hope the other
medical students aren't sad because they
didn't get a toy with their cadaver, too.

(Steve Young)

The Top 17 Signs You're the Reincarnation of Someone Famous

17. Working on your back under the car, you get the sudden urge to paint a church.

16. Same thing every morning: wake up, brush teeth, carve "SID" into your chest with a razor blade.

15. You can actually sing *Bohemian Rhapsody* without sounding like a complete idiot.

14. When your boss criticizes your efforts, you hack off your ear.

13. Disqualified during swimsuit competition for smoking cigar and wiggling eyebrows at other contestants.

12. You've got Bette Davis eyes.

11. Can't understand why a fine physician like yourself is being sued for applying leeches to a patient.

10. Century after century, you find Shirley MacLaine annoying.

9. Not only do you consider Yoko an artistic genius, you *love* her singing voice.

8. Whenever you get sick, it's always a rockin' pneumonia or a boogie-woogie flu.

7. In preparation for Hurricane Hortense, you build a giant boat and start stealing your neighbors' pets.

6. When you wake up in a puddle of your own overdose-induced vomit, you find yourself inexplicably crying out for Mr. French.

5. You cannot tell a lie. Nevertheless, you're running for president.

4. Other Boy Scouts return from that first mountain hike with poison ivy; *you're* lugging tablets of inscribed stone.

3. You soil your pants when you hear the words, "Little Bighorn."

2. Timmy is stuck in the old mine and all you can do is bark as your husband asks, "What is it, girl?!?"

1. That six-figure advance for your book, *I Was the Pelvis*, buys a shitload of deep-fried peanut-butter-and-banana sandwiches.

The list on the preceding page is from September 16, 1996.
It was compiled from 82 submissions from 25 contributors.

Jennifer Ritzinger, Seattle, WA	– 1, 9
Bruce Ansley, Baltimore, MD	– 1, 9
Matt Diamond, Holland, PA	– 1
Dee Anne Phillips, Shreveport, LA	– 2, 13
Greg Sadosuk, Fairfax, VA	– 2
Don Horton, Sacramento, CA	– 3
Kathleen Buchanan, Tuscaloosa, AL	– 4, 12
Gene Markins-Dieden, New Haven, CT	– 5
Caroline Gennity, Virginia Beach, VA	– 6
Paul Paternoster, Redwood City, CA	– 7
Kim Moser, New York, NY	– 8
Kermit Woodall, Richmond, VA	– 10
Lee Oeth, San Diego, CA	– 10
David W. James, Los Angeles, CA	– 11
Jennifer Hart, Arlington, VA	– 14
Joel McClure, Sterling Heights, MI	– 15
Jeffrey House, Detroit, MI	– 16, Topic
Doug Johnson, Santa Cruz, CA	– 17

During job interviews, when they
ask, "What is your worst quality?"
I always say, "Flatulence."
That way I get my own office.

(Dan Thompson)

I'm hoping I can get my share of the multi-million-dollar tobacco lawsuit settlement in Camel Cash, 'cause I could really use a bitchin' Camel backpack.

(George MacMillan)

The Top 17 Signs You're at a Bad Renaissance Festival

17. The castle and village are made entirely of Legos.

16. Turkey leg bears striking resemblance to cocker spaniel leg.

15. Festival activities include "Ye Olde Wet T-Shirt Contest."

14. Eight-minute drum solo in the middle of *Greensleeves*.

13. "Belly up to the bar, me lad, for some grilled mahi-mahi and fresh California roll!"

12. Ye Olde Glassblower makes nothing but crack pipes.

11. The mead is served in a coconut shell with a fizzy straw.

10. Everyone seems to have attended the Kevin Costner School of British Accents.

9. Mosh pit follows the wandering minstrels.

8. You get charged 5 bucks to take a leak behind Ye Olde Hedge.

7. Guillotine exhibit closed due to pending litigation.

6. Friar Tuck's pager keeps going off.

5. Featured event: Johnson jousting!

4. Disgusting ogre is merely an unshaved Marlon Brando.

3. "Tarry, wench, I prithee! Wouldst thou Macarena?"

2. Merlin the Magician's only trick is "Got your nose!"

1. Jousting Crips & Bloods

The list on the preceding page is from September 25, 1996. It was compiled from 141 submissions by 40 contributors.

John Voigt, Chicago, IL	– 1, 13
Lloyd Jacobson, Washington, DC	– 1
Bill Muse, Seattle, WA	– 2
Matt Diamond, Holland, PA	– 3
Stephen Pace, Houston, TX	– 4
Kim Moser, New York, NY	– 5
David G. Scott, Kansas City, MO	– 6
Paul Paternoster, Redwood City, CA	– 7
Jennifer Hart, Arlington, VA	– 8
Craig Stacey, St. Paul, MN	– 9
Lev L. Spiro, Los Angeles, CA	– 10
Chuck Smith, Woodbridge, VA	– 11
Marshal Perlman, Minneapolis, MN	– 12, Topic
George Olson, Colorado Springs, CO	– 14
Jeff Downey, Raleigh, NC	– 15
Greg Pettit, Houston, TX	– 16
Glenn Marcus, Washington, DC	– 17

If there are two sides to every story, why do supermarket tabloids always give the benefit of the doubt to the space aliens?

(Doug Johnson)

The one really important thing to remember about juggling meat cleavers is that if you get a funny feeling that you're suddenly juggling more things than you started off with, it's time to start counting fingers.

(Andy Ihnatko)

The Top 15 Complaints
of Modern-Day Vampires

15. Goth look makes it difficult to tell living from the undead.

14. Nutrasweet or not, fat-free blood tastes like crap.

13. Hard to get a decent puncture with latex on your fangs.

12. Three words: daylight saving time

11. Can't enjoy a meal at Burger King without some redneck yelling, "Look, Ma! It's Elvis!"

10. After 45 years of Communist rule, it's impossible to find clean, uncontaminated Transylvanian soil for bottom of coffin.

9. After 100 years of trying, still can't score with Elvira.

8. No bat is safe with Ozzy Osbourne around.

7. With all those crucifix-wearing Madonna clones, junior highs are suddenly off-limits.

6. No warm blood for miles around DC.

5. Exhausted from all those Calvin Klein photo shoots.

4. No small task beating F. Lee Bailey to a warm body.

3. Buxom wenches of old have been replaced by aerobicized "hardbodies."

2. Baboon heart makes everything taste gamey.

1. Sick and tired of being mistaken for Keith Richards.

The list on the preceding page is from October 23, 1996. It was compiled from 144 submissions by 41 contributors.

George Olson, Colorado Springs, CO	– 1, 5, 7
John Voigt, Chicago, IL	– 2
Christopher Troise, New York, NY	– 3
Ed Brooksbank, Sacramento, CA	– 4
Marc Cukier, Toronto, Canada	– 4
Greg Pettit, Houston, TX	– 4
Joel McClure, Sterling Heights, MI	– 6, 13
Tom Louderback, Breckenridge, CO	– 7, 10
Jennifer Ritzinger, Seattle, WA	– 8, 14
Bruce Ansley, Baltimore, MD	– 9
Jeff Downey, Raleigh, NC	– 11
Lev L. Spiro, Los Angeles, CA	– 12
Sam Evans, Charleston, SC	– 12
Greg Sadosuk, Fairfax, VA	– 13
Kim Moser, New York, NY	– 13
Eric Huret, Atlanta, GA	– 14
Don Horton, Sacramento, CA	– 14
David W. James, Los Angeles, CA	– 15
Paul Paternoster, Redwood City, CA	– Topic

As I lay there fighting for my last breath, racked by pain, unable to move, I realized that indeed there are some things *not* worth dying for... so I ditched the WonderCorset.

(Anna L. Juarez)

I'm going back to that diner often, because the waitress obviously has a crush on me. I can tell because she calls me "hon" when she takes my order.

(Tom Sims)

The Top 16 Signs Your Cat Is Overweight

16. Cat door retrofitted with garage door opener.

15. Confused guests constantly mistaking her for a beanbag chair.

14. Always lands on her spleen.

13. Fewer calls to the fire department, but a sudden upsurge in broken branches.

12. Fifteen-month gestation period, and still no kittens.

11. No longer cleans itself unless coated in Cheez Whiz.

10. Anna Nicole Smith fits through your kitty door without the aid of lubricants.

9. Cat food dish replaced with Rush Limbaugh trough.

8. Luxurious, shiny black fur replaced with mint-green polyester pants suit.

7. It's no longer safe to lift him without a spotter.

6. "Steals breath" from all five quintuplets, simultaneously.

5. Larry King keeps trying to kiss it full on the lips.

4. Waits for the third bowl of food to get finicky.

3. Only catches mice that get trapped in his gravitational pull.

2. Enormous gut keeps your hardwood floors freshly buffed.

1. Has more chins than lives.

The list on the preceding page is from November 8, 1996. It was compiled from 117 submissions by 38 contributors.

Bill Muse, Seattle, WA	– 1, 2, 16
Doug Johnson, Santa Cruz, CA	– 2, 16
Greg Sadosuk, Fairfax, VA	– 2, 15
Paul Paternoster, Redwood City, CA	– 3, Topic
Lee Oeth, San Diego, CA	– 3
David W. James, Los Angeles, CA	– 4
Craig Stacey, St. Paul, MN	– 5
Jeffrey House, Detroit, MI	– 6
Caroline Gennity, Virginia Beach, VA	– 7, 15
Blair Bostick, Alexandria, VA	– 8
Matt Alford, Salem, OR	– 9
Sterling Smith, Houston, TX	– 10
John Voigt, Chicago, IL	– 11
Tisha Stacey, St. Paul, MN	– 12
Dee Anne Phillips, Shreveport, LA	– 13
Matt Diamond, Holland, PA	– 13
George Olson, Colorado Springs, CO	– 14
R.M. Weiner, Brighton MA	– 15
Chuck Smith, Woodbridge, VA	– 16

It's a good thing that a freak time warp hasn't swapped Leonardo DiCaprio and Leonardo da Vinci, because I'm not sure I could handle seeing both a naked Mona Lisa *and* a smirking Kate Winslet.

(Chris Lipe)

Women keep accusing me of mentally undressing them with my eyes. They couldn't be more wrong; I'm actually mentally undressing them with my hands and teeth.

(Trevor Green)

The Top 15 Signs You Read Too Many Comic Books

15. More than a little disappointed you didn't get invited to Superman's wedding.

14. Keep memorizing words like "SSPPLLAATT," "KAPOW" and "BLAMMMMO" for school spelling bee.

13. Your resume lists your last three jobs as Defender of the Galaxy, Sidekick to Defender of the Galaxy, and Assistant Manager of Inter-Galactic 7-Eleven.

12. You shout "Curses! Foiled again!" when they forget the catsup at the drive-through.

11. You whack your boss over the head with a hammer and are surprised when his head doesn't pop back into shape.

10. Despite repeated attempts to stop speeding cars with your bare hands, neighbors still think you're just a suicidal lunatic.

9. At age 43, you set the state subscription record for Grit Magazine.

8. Your compulsive self-narrative renders you too transparent for a career in real estate or car repair.

7. You're the only one wearing a cape at step aerobics.

6. "Holy 40-year-old virgin, Batman!"

5. Wife is tired of you introducing her as "my trusty sidekick."

4. Most of your sick days are due to "the effects of the earth's yellow sun."

3. Refusing to admit you're drunk, you vow revenge on your evil arch-enemy "Flaccidus" for your inability to perform in bed.

2. Your secret identity keeps drinking all the beer.

1. Your attempts at becoming "Danger Cloud" are proving hard on the underwear.

The list on the preceding page is from November 20, 1996.
It was compiled from 103 submissions by 39 contributors.

David W. James, Los Angeles, CA	– 1, 12
Greg Pettit, Houston, TX	– 2
Caroline Gennity, Virginia Beach, VA	– 3
George Olson, Colorado Springs, CO	– 4
Jeffrey House, Detroit, MI	– 5, 10
Tisha Stacey, St. Paul, MN	– 6
Joel McClure, Sterling Heights, MI	– 7
LeMel Hebert-Williams, San Francisco, CA	– 8
David Hyatt, New York, NY	– 9
Michael Migdol, Osaka, Japan	– 11
Meredith Ogden, Ithaca, NY	– 13
Lev L. Spiro, Los Angeles, CA	– 14
Greg Sadosuk, Fairfax, VA	– 14
Jeff Downey, Raleigh, NC	– 15
David G. Scott, Kansas City, MO	– Topic

You know that old public-speaking trick
of picturing your audience naked?
I like to pretend they're on fire.
That way, it makes a lot more sense
when I run screaming from the stage.

(Craig Stacey)

It was bad enough when I discovered my
girlfriend could bait a hook better than
I can, but when she used a "Curly Sideways-Hand"
to block my "Moe Two-Finger Eye-Poke," I really
began to wonder if "she" used to be a "he."

(Clynch Varnadore)

The Top 17 Signs the Santa at the Mall Is Nuts

17. Shaves head and beard, then insists on being called "Santa Kurtz."
16. Tells kids about the comparative kill ratio of the AK-47 over the Daisy air rifle.
15. Those nasty chewing-tobacco streaks in his beard.
14. Has a complimentary tray of North Pole "tundra oysters" ready for the toddlers.
13. After every child's request, asks, "Wouldn't you rather have a nice big bag of clams?"
12. The twinkle in his eye and the twitch of his nose are due to a lack of medication.
11. Every so often, snaps into a Slim Jim and growls, "You've been bad and now you're going down, punk!"
10. Promises children O.J. will be cleared of all wrongdoing.
9. Caught drinking red wine with fish during break.
8. "Hey kid, bet I can wet my pants faster than you can!"
7. Insists on blowing his nose in children's hair.
6. Despite massive photographic evidence to the contrary, claims to have never worn white gloves or shiny black boots.
5. That snowy beard? Nothin' but nose hair.
4. Answers every child's toy request with, "Dream on, peewee!"
3. Enjoys it so much when small children urinate on his lap, he happily returns the favor.
2. Instead of a candy cane, gives each kid a pack of Marlboros and a homemade venison pie.
1. While it's admittedly a nifty trick, blowing smoke rings out of his tracheotomy hole is just scaring the hell out of the kiddies.

The list on the preceding page is from December 30, 1997.
It was compiled from 132 submissions from 47 contributors.

Caroline Gennity, Virginia Beach, VA	– 1, 11
Rob Seulowitz, New York, NY	– 2
Kermit Woodall, Richmond, VA	– 2
John Hering, Alexandria, VA	– 2
Sterling Smith, Houston, TX	– 3
Jeffrey House, Detroit, MI	– 3
Bill Muse, Seattle, WA	– 4
Mitch Patterson, Atlanta, GA	– 5
Meredith Ogden, Ithaca, NY	– 6
David W. James, Los Angeles, CA	– 7
Blair Bostick, Alexandria, VA	– 8
Rob Winchell, Arlington, MA	– 9
Jay Allen, Santa Barbara, CA	– 10
Ed Smith, Chattanooga, TN	– 12
Tisha Stacey, St. Paul, MN	– 13
Chuck Smith, Woodbridge, VA	– 14
Chris White, New York, NY	– 15
Lloyd Jacobson, Washington, DC	– 16
Jeff Downey, Raleigh, NC	– 17
Jennifer Ritzinger, Seattle, WA	– Topic

Sometimes I just stare at my computer screen
and wonder what technology hath wrought.
Other times I stare at it and think,
"Those have *got* to be fake."

(Gregor Young)

My wife says I'm not ambitious enough.
I suppose I could find someone
more supportive, but why bother?

(Jim Rosenberg)

Incest isn't really so bad, as long as
you only do it with other people's sisters.

(J.D. Smith)

"What Would Jesus Do?" isn't as helpful
as you'd think when your wife catches
you wearing her clothes and makeup.

(Bob Van Voris)

My colleagues accuse me of being a pothead because
I'm a Libertarian. All I have to say about that is
this: You gotta check out the NASA channel right
now, totally, 'cause I swear that Argentina is moving
really slowly to the west. Seriously! Oh, man.

(Mark Niebuhr)

If the FDA really cared about *everyone*, they
would make children wear nutrition labels so
witches could make healthy food descisions as well.

(Davejames)

I would hate to be an ant: crowded living
conditions and non-stop work, and then one kid
with a magnifying glass ruins your whole day.

(Brad Osberg)

They say that unless you're the lead dog,
the view never changes. However, if
you actually were a dog, you would
probably prefer that other view.

(Dave Davies)

So why can't they make *tampons*
that are ribbed for my pleasure?

(Jenni Elion)

I think you and your spouse should share
the pressures and burdens in your lives.
But don't let your co-workers find out,
because not everyone approves of cross-stressing.

(Mark Weiss)

At the end of the day, my boss always
says, "Another day, another dollar."
And I thought *I* was underpaid.

(Maurizio Mariotti)

I bet strip mining is a lot like strip
poker, only the last thing you take off
is that helmet with the light on it.

(Steve Oglesby)

The Top 15 Dr. Seuss Pick-Up Lines

15. "I may not like green ham or eggs,
    But I sure love your long, thin legs."

14. "Marvin K. Mooney, will you please come now?!?"

13. "From far or near or here or there,
    Haven't I seen you before somewhere?"

12. "That's not the only place this Sneetch has a star, baby."

11. "Sally from Whoville, what's your sign?
    Let's blow this joint... your thneed or mine?"

10. "Y'know, after he stole it, the Grinch hid Christmas... in my pants."

9. "I love someone who knows what wine goes with red fish or blue fish."

8. "Is that a cat in your hat or are you just happy to see me?"

7. "I hate this place — the crowd's so phony!
   Say, care to ride me like a pony?"

6. "My heart ain't the only thing two sizes too large, if you know what I mean."

5. "On a boat, in a car, with your toes all curled,
   Oh, the places we'll go when I rock your world!"

4. "How'd you like to be in my next book, *Great Legs and Ass*?"

3. "I do not like my wife, you see.
   I do not like her, no sirree.
   Her looks accuse, her words disparage,
   And so we have this open marriage."

2. "Each book makes a million, a zillion or three.
   Would you, could you, come home with me?"

1. "In all of Hooterville, where there's Hooters supreme,
   Yours are the best of the Hooters I've seen!"

The list on the preceding page is from December 11, 1996. It was compiled from 118 submissions from 45 contributors.

Dee Anne Phillips, Shreveport, LA	– 1
Ed Smith, Chattanooga, TN	– 2
George Olson, Colorado Springs, CO	– 3
Bill Muse, Seattle, WA	– 4
Brad Schreiber, Los Angeles, CA	– 5
Lisa Stepaniak, Dearborn, MI	– 6
Caroline Gennity, Virginia Beach, VA	– 7
Craig Stacey, St. Paul, MN	– 8
Paul Seaburn, Houston, TX	– 9
Alexander Clemens, San Francisco, CA	– 10
Tony Hill, Minneapolis, MN	– 11
Jennifer Ritzinger, Seattle, WA	– 11
David W. James, Los Angeles, CA	– 12
Norman Kenney, Carlsbad, CA	– 13
David Hyatt, New York, NY	– 14
Blair Bostick, Alexandria, VA	– 15
Robert P. Mader, Knoxville, TN	– Topic

One day Grandma tried to pinch my cheeks so I turned my head, snapped my jaws and bit off her fingers. I don't think she'll be trying that for a while.

(Anna Chin-Williams)

Nobody seemed to care when I came home and shouted the good news: "I got the part! I got the part!" Makes me think I should have been an actor instead of a mechanic.

(J. Hutter)

The Top 16 Signs Your Grandmother May Be a Serial Killer

16. That afghan she's been knitting? One hundred percent human hair.

15. Bone fragments in her mincemeat pies.

14. A sudden fondness for serving figgy pudding, while Mr. Figgy down the road has been missing for over a week.

13. Complains that her freezer just doesn't have enough headroom.

12. Trash bags of "rose clippings" are awfully damn heavy and smell like hell.

11. Her collection of antique thimbles includes thumbs.

10. After every evening homicide report, carves another notch in the arm of her rocker.

9. Doesn't serve crab Louie on Melba toast – serves Louie and Melba.

8. Arrives at her own surgery with replacement organs in hand.

7. Mistakenly served her bridge club actual lady fingers.

6. You've never heard of a church that has midnight mass *every* night.

5. Nothing to show for her six marriages except a well-stocked freezer.

4. You don't get homemade chicken noodle soup; you get head-of-the-kid-next-door-who-wouldn't-turn-his-radio-down-soup.

3. Has a bumper sticker that reads, "Ask me about my latest victim."

2. Just a funny feeling you get when she's in her room with the lights off and *Helter Skelter* turned up full blast on the ol' Victrola.

1. Accidentally sends you her manifesto and mails a letter about her hip replacement to the *Washington Post*.

The list on the preceding page is from December 18, 1996.
It was compiled from 98 submissions from 36 contributors.

Meredith Ogden, Ithaca, NY	– 1
Ed Smith, Chattanooga, TN	– 2, 3
Mitch Patterson, Atlanta, GA	– 2, 7
Chris White, New York, NY	– 3, 6
Jennifer Ritzinger, Seattle, WA	– 4
Alexander Clemens, San Francisco, CA	– 5, 16
Caroline Gennity, Virginia Beach, VA	– 5, Topic
Ed Brooksbank, Sacramento, CA	– 5
Jennifer Bieneman, Grand Rapids, MI	– 6
Sterling Smith, Houston, TX	– 7
Greg Pettit, Houston, TX	– 7
Bill Muse, Seattle, WA	– 7
Matt Alford, Salem, OR	– 8
Gene Markins-Dieden, New Haven, CT	– 9
Doug Johnson, Santa Cruz, CA	– 10
LeMel Hebert-Williams, San Fran., CA	– 11
Marianne Tatom, Austin, TX	– 12
Bob Mader, Knoxville TN	– 13
Craig Stacey, St. Paul, MN	– 14
Tom Louderback, Breckenridge, CO	– 15
John Voigt, Chicago, IL	– 16
Bruce Ansley, Baltimore, MD	– 16

If I had a dog, I'd train him to kill on command.
And the command I'd use would be "Is he friendly?"

(R.M. Weiner)

Sometimes I lie in bed at night
and think of all the stuff in the world.
Hoo boy, there's a bunch of it.

(Brian Auten)

The Top 14 Threats Used in Dysfunctional Families

14. "Finish your lima beans or you're not getting any heroin for dessert!"

13. "If you don't stop that this instant, I'll have Grandma perform another striptease for you."

12. "If this Plexiglas weren't between us, I'd wash your mouth out with soap, young man."

11. "Do you want me to put a tofu burrito in your pants? Well? Do you?!"

10. "Billy Bob, you finish them chores or Sis ain't goin' to the prom with ya!"

9. "Eat your Brussels sprouts, or Mommy won't love you anymore."

8. "Lyle, Erik — either behave or go to your suites!"

7. "If you don't eat your peas, Chelsea, I'll make you stay at the Gingriches' house!"

6. "Don't make me put you back in the womb!"

5. "As long as you live under this roof, you're *going* to wear that dress, young man!"

4. "You just wait till your father gets paroled!"

3. "Stop crying, Lourdes, or Uncle Dennis will kick you in the groin."

2. "Young lady, don't make me send you to the Citadel!"

1. "All right, little mister, no more time in the sheep pen for you!"

The list on the preceding page is from January 27, 1997.
It was compiled from 121 submissions from 41 contributors.

Debbie Lander, Las Vegas, NV	– 1, 10
Paul Seaburn, Houston, TX	– 2
Bill Muse, Seattle, WA	– 3
Steve Hurd, San Ramon, CA	– 4
Jeffrey House, Detroit, MI	– 5
Craig Stacey, St. Paul, MN	– 5
David W. James, Los Angeles, CA	– 6
Bruce Ansley, Baltimore, MD	– 7
Blair Bostick, Alexandria, VA	– 8
Marianne Tatom, Austin, TX	– 9
Rob Winchell, Arlington, MA	– 11
John Voigt, Chicago, IL	– 12
Tisha Stacey, St. Paul, MN	– 13
Christopher Troise, New York, NY	– 13
Caroline Gennity, Virginia Beach, VA	– 14
Jonathan Jermey, Blaxland, Australia	– Topic

If you ever get pulled over by a police officer
and he says, "Where's the fire?" you should say,
"At my house!" then speed off. Just remember
to call ahead and have someone start a fire at
your house, or you'll end up in mighty big trouble.

(Jason Brewer)

The thing I don't get about *Davey
and Goliath* is that with all of
the talk about God and the Bible
and everything, no one stopped to
notice the miracle of the talking dog.

(Meaghan O'Malley)

The Top 12 Things You Don't Want to Hear From Tech Support

12. "Do you have a sledgehammer or a brick handy?"

11. "That's right — not even MacGyver could fix it."

10. "So, what are you wearing?"

9. "Duuuuuude! Bummer!"

8. "Looks like you're gonna need some new dilithium crystals, Cap'n."

7. "Press 1 for support.
    Press 2 if you're with *60 Minutes*.
    Press 3 if you're with the FTC."

6. "We can fix this, but you're gonna need a butter knife, a roll of duct tape and a car battery."

5. "I'm sorry, Dave. I'm afraid I can't do that."

4. "In layman's terms, we call that the Hindenburg effect."

3. "Hold on a second... Mom! Timmy's hitting me!"

2. "Okay, turn to page 523 in your copy of *Dianetics*."

1. "Please hold for Mr. Gates' attorney."

The list on the preceding page is from January 28, 1997. It was compiled from 83 submissions from 31 contributors.

George Olson, Colorado Springs, CO	– 1
R.M. Weiner, Brighton, MA	– 2
John Voigt, Chicago, IL	– 3, 10
Chris White, New York, NY	– 4, 8
Jeff Downey, Raleigh, NC	– 5
Caroline Gennity, Virginia Beach, VA	– 6, 10
Kermit Woodall, Richmond, VA	– 7
Alexander Clemens, San Francisco, CA	– 9
Jennifer Ritzinger, Seattle, WA	– 10
David W. James, Los Angeles, CA	– 11
Bob Mader, Knoxville TN	– 12
Chris White, New York, NY	– Topic

Whoever said the hand is quicker
than the eye obviously never tried
rolling them both down a ramp.

(Paul Paternoster)

When I hear about 8-year-old kids working
20 hours a day in factories overseas, I think
to myself, "Damn, if they have a 401(k) plan,
they'll be able to retire when they're 30!"

(Scott E. Frank)

If I were depressed and lazy,
I'd commit suicide by old age.

(Pam Pickard)

The Top 15 Signs Your Dog Has a Problem With Alcohol

15. Wakes up looking for a little hair o' the human who bit him.

14. Won't go near that darn chuck wagon, but when the bar cart rolls through, he's off like a shot.

13. Lately you've noticed that he'll even hump a really *ugly* leg.

12. No matter what you throw for him to fetch, always returns with a bottle of Cuervo and a lime.

11. Chases pink elephants around the yard instead of squirrels.

10. The only game she'll play with you is Quarters.

9. Spends more time hugging the toilet bowl than actually slurping from it.

8. Sells house, moves to Vegas, shacks up with beautiful hooker.

7. Justifies quantities consumed by reasoning that they are in "dog beers."

6. When he hikes his leg at the fireplug he keeps falling over backward.

5. Won't drink out of the toilet unless there's an olive in it.

4. Just signed to do a remake of *Old Yeller* with Kelsey Grammer and Robert Downey, Jr.

3. After a few too many at the office party, tries to pick up the boss's bitch.

2. "Ri *ruv* you, man!!!"

1. He used to bark — now he just belches the chorus to "Louie, Louie."

The list on the preceding page is from February 12, 1997. It was compiled from 137 submissions from 50 contributors.

Alexander Clemens, San Francisco, CA	– 1
Christopher Troise, New York, NY	– 2
Michael Wolf, Brookline, MA	– 2
David G. Scott, Kansas City, MO	– 3
Paul Seaburn, Houston, TX	– 4, 5
Jennifer Ritzinger, Seattle, WA	– 4
George Olson, Colorado Springs, CO	– 4
Chuck Smith, Woodbridge, VA	– 4
Ed Smith, Chattanooga, TN	– 6
Patrick New, Chicago, IL	– 7
Jeff Downey, Raleigh, NC	– 8
Wade Kwon, Birmingham, AL	– 9, 15
Lloyd Jacobson, Washington, DC	– 9
R.M. Weiner, Brighton, MA	– 10
Marianne Tatom, Austin, TX	– 11
Jeffrey House, Detroit, MI	– 12
Gail Celio, Athens, GA	– 12
Bill Gray, Waterloo, ON, Canada	– 13
Bruce Ansley, Baltimore, MD	– 13
Mitch Patterson, Atlanta, GA	– 13
Jim Louderback, Boston, MA	– 14
Peg Warner, Derry, NH	– 15
Blair Bostick, Alexandria, VA	– 15
Debbie Lander, Las Vegas, NV	– Topic

If they made the game where you flush
the toilet halfway through urinating, then try
to time the end of the flush with the end
of your urination so as to not get any urine
into the fresh water, into an Olympic event...
I bet I wouldn't even place, 'cause man,
I just ain't no good at that game.

(George MacMillan)

The Top 15 Signs You're Being Stalked by Martha Stewart

15. Mysterious late-night phone calls: "I can't stop thinking about you... and that's a good thing!"

14. Contents of your curbside recycling tub stolen and replaced with juice-can pencil holders and milk carton flower vases.

13. On her show she makes a gingerbread house that looks exactly like your split-level, right down to the fallen-over licorice downspout and the stuck-half-open graham cracker garage door.

12. You get a threatening note made up of letters cut out of a magazine with pinking shears, and they're all the same size, the same font, and precisely lined up in razor-sharp rows.

11. Size 6 Bruno Magli imprints on all your doilies.

10. You find your pet bunny on the stove in an exquisite tarragon, rose petal and saffron demi-glace, with pecan-crusted hearts of palm and a delicate mint-fennel sauce.

9. The unmistakable aroma of potpourri follows you — even after you leave the bathroom.

8. You discover that every napkin in the whole friggin' house has been folded into a swan.

7. No matter *where* you eat, your place setting always includes an oyster fork.

6. Annoying crank phone calls begin with, "Hold, please, for Ms. Stewart."

5. Twice this week you've been the victim of a drive-by doilying.

4. That telltale lemon slice in the dog's water bowl.

3. The sharpened macaroni shells underfoot in the bathroom are stained to match the shower curtain.

2. You wake up in the hospital with a concussion and endive stuffing in every orifice.

1. You awaken one morning with a glue gun pointed squarely at your temple.

The list on the preceding page is from March 11, 1997.
It was compiled from 126 submissions from 43 contributors.

Jeff Downey, Raleigh, NC	– 1, Topic
Caroline Gennity, Virginia Beach, VA	– 2
Kris Johnson, Burbank, CA	– 3
Barbara Rush, Tulsa, OK	– 4
Paul Paternoster, Redwood City, CA	– 5
Marsha Clodfelter, Corpus Christi, TX	– 6
Don Horton, Sacramento, CA	– 7
Jennifer Ritzinger, Seattle, WA	– 8
R.M. Weiner, Brighton, MA	– 8
Bruce Ansley, Baltimore, MD	– 9
Greg Pettit, Houston, TX	– 9
Blair Bostick, Alexandria, VA	– 10
Natasha Filipovic, New York, NY	– 10
Steve Hurd, San Ramon, CA	– 10
Bob Mader, Knoxville TN	– 10
Dee Anne Phillips, Shreveport, LA	– 10
Lev L. Spiro, Los Angeles, CA	– 10
Bruce Ansley, Baltimore, MD	– 11
Chris Gleason, Germantown, MD	– 12
David Hyatt, New York, NY	– 12
Bill Muse, Seattle, WA	– 13
Gail Celio, Athens, GA	– 14
Craig Stacey, St. Paul, MN	– 14
Kate d'Oliveira, Ft. Lauderdale, FL	– 15

If I ever get married, I think it would be
funny to hire a stuntwoman to run through
the church in a burning wedding dress.
Then I would put her out with a bottle of
seltzer and everyone would have a good laugh.
I'm having kind of a hard time
finding a girlfriend, though.

(Bob Van Voris)

The Top 15 Side Effects of the Female Orgasm Pill

15. Forget your anniversary? No problem. Forget to stop at the pharmacy? Kiss your sorry ass good-bye.

14. More huge smiles and dazed looks than at a Moonie mass wedding.

13. Entire male population puts on their Nikes, knits a purple shroud, and sits down for a nice lunch of applesauce and vodka.

12. Spiking the punch *really* shakes things up at the senior prom.

11. The president finds he has much more time to deny allegations.

10. Senator Orrin Hatch withdraws constitutional amendment to ban pill after a good ass-kicking from Mrs. Hatch.

9. Undertakers working overtime to wipe those smiles off.

8. Severe sales slump forces the Energizer bunny to look for work elsewhere.

7. Finally, after several decades — a new topic for country-western songs!

6. The Betty Ford Clinic adds a new wing.

5. Due to unexpected flashbacks, housewives everywhere are being banned from the supermarket.

4. Porno movie casts pared down to a woman and a glass of water.

3. "Hi, handsome. The bartender tells me you're a pharmacist."

2. "Coming, Mother!" takes on a whole new meaning.

1. Janet Reno cracks a smile.

The list on the preceding page is from April 18, 1997.
It was compiled from 107 submissions from 41 contributors.

Doug Johnson, Santa Cruz, CA	– 1, 6
Mitch Patterson, Atlanta, GA	– 1
Kermit Woodall, Richmond, VA	– 1
Paul Schindler, Orinda, CA	– 2
Jonathan Cook, Madison, WI	– 3
Matt Loiselle, Detroit, MI	– 4, 11
Debbie Lander, Las Vegas, NV	– 5
Steve Hurd, San Ramon, CA	– 6, 14
Chuck Smith, Woodbridge, VA	– 6
Matt Diamond, Holland, PA	– 7
Matt Alford, Portland, OR	– 8
Paul Seaburn, Houston, TX	– 9
Jeff Downey, Raleigh, NC	– 10
Lev L. Spiro, Los Angeles, CA	– 12
Paul Paternoster, Redwood City, CA	– 13
Alexander Clemens, San Francisco, CA	– 13
Caroline Gennity, Virginia Beach, VA	– 15
Bruce Ansley, Baltimore, MD	– Topic

Thirty-six years ago I wished upon a star.
Today, the Thumbelina doll I asked
for finally showed up. And you know
what that means? I'M GETTIN' A PONY!!!

(Anne Sholl)

Sure, it may sound pathetic that I spent
Valentine's Day home alone with a bottle of wine,
listening to "One is the Loneliest Number" over
and over again. But hey, at least I got lucky.

(Silas Knight)

The Top 15 Signs Your Company's Diversity Program Isn't Working

15. Diversity = white guys with red necks.

14. Three months after your written request, your cellblock guards are still 100 percent male.

13. To meet state-mandated diversity ratios, company offers a raise to anyone willing to be gay one week a month.

12. Crazy Serbs in marketing just can't get along with wacky Bosnians in accounting.

11. Featured film on movie night: *Amos 'n' Andy Meet Charlie Chan*

10. Sudden unexplained increase in the number of *Dukes of Hazzard* cars in the parking lot.

9. Human Resources places an ad that reads: "Wanted: a Black, a Jew, an Oriental and two broads."

8. Co-workers refer to you as "The Diversity Babe."

7. You're named 1997 Company of the Year by Aryan Brotherhood Today magazine.

6. Only black face seen lately was when CEO did Al Jolson impression at the annual shareholders meeting.

5. You work at Confederate Flags Is Us.

4. Looking back, organizing that "spin the dreidel" game at the Kwanzaa party was probably a bad idea.

3. Multicultural luncheon features White Trash Casserole Starch Surprise.

2. Company has Celtics season tickets, even though the office is in downtown Boise.

1. Your law firm's name? Schott, Zoeller, Fuhrman and Helms.

The list on the preceding page is from April 24, 1997.
It was compiled from 120 submissions from 44 contributors.

Too many contributors to list	– 1
Don Horton, Sacramento, CA	– 2
Marianne Tatom, Austin, TX	– 3
Jesse Garon, San Francisco, CA	– 4
David Hyatt, New York, NY	– 5
Steve Hurd, San Ramon, CA	– 6
Jeff Downey, Raleigh, NC	– 6
Ed Smith, Chattanooga, TN	– 7
Matt Loiselle, Detroit, MI	– 8
Kim Moser, New York, NY	– 9
Sterling Smith, Houston, TX	– 10
Glenn Marcus, Washington, DC	– 11
Lev L. Spiro, Los Angeles, CA	– 12
Bill Muse, Seattle, WA	– 13
Jeffrey House, Detroit, MI	– 13
Matt Diamond, Holland, PA	– 14
Sam Evans, Charleston, SC	– 15
David G. Scott, Kansas City, MO	– Topic

Word to the wise: Most bosses only fall for
the old "pencil through the eyeball, so I have to
go to the hospital" trick once. But if you time
it right, you can get a long weekend out of it.

(Lynn Pruett)

I've heard it said that your worst day when
you're alive is better than your best day
when you're dead. Personally, I think that's
just a bunch of crap that dead people say.

(Jeremy Swiller)

The Top 15 Signs You're Not Graduating This Term

15. You planned on being there, but they moved the trial to Denver.

14. You're on a football scholarship at Oklahoma.

13. You get a snide letter from admissions recommending a summer course in Remedial Tuition Payment.

12. You don't feel you've yet done sufficient field research on your thesis topic: "The Munchies: What Causes Them?"

11. You spent over $400 on new books this semester, but over $40,000 on beer and pizza.

10. Final: "Calculate the load-bearing capacity of a bituminous concrete mix."
    You: Calculated the vomit-producing capacity of mixing tequila and beer the night before the exam.

9. NBC and CBS feature live, round-the-clock coverage of your frat dorm.

8. You won the Heisman, the Nike commercial shoot is tomorrow and you haven't been to class since late November.

7. Six years of college and all you've learned are the lyrics to "Louie, Louie."

6. Your cap and gown are made of paper and have CAMPUS FOOD SERVICE written on them.

5. You're still an undergrad, but the faculty grants you tenure.

4. Your blood-alcohol level is consistently higher than your GPA.

3. Only sheepskin you'll see this summer is in the barn.

2. Your tassel makes up half of your work uniform.

1. You got all A's, but your name is Hester Prynne.

The list on the preceding page is from May 29, 1997.
It was compiled from 110 submissions from 40 contributors.

Glenn Marcus, Washington, DC	– 1
Marsha Clodfelter, Corpus Christi, TX	– 2, 3
Dave George, Arlington, VA	– 2
Fred Hesby, Portland, OR	– 4, 6
John Hering, Alexandria, VA	– 4
Gene Markins-Dieden, New Haven, CT	– 5
Kevin Freels, Sun Valley, CA	– 6
Jeff Downey, Raleigh, NC	– 7
Rob Seulowitz, New York, NY	– 8
Kim Moser, New York, NY	– 9
Peg Warner, Derry, NH	– 10
Tisha Stacey, Lisle, IL	– 11
Alexander Clemens, San Francisco, CA	– 12
Lev L. Spiro, Los Angeles, CA	– 13
David G. Scott, Kansas City, MO	– 14
Ed Smith, Chattanooga, TN	– 15
Paul Paternoster, Redwood City, CA	– Topic

Everything I needed to know about
life, I learned in kindergarten:
If you go to the bathroom in your
pants, they let you go home.

(Anthony Myers)

Who knew the cars following that hearse weren't part of the parade? I may have been a little out of place in my Patches the Clown outfit, but at least the mourners seemed to enjoy my dancing-with-a-cadaver act.

(Stephanie Thompson)

If I were a leprechaun, I would use the lure
of my pot of gold to pick up hot chicks.
But the joke would be on them, because I
would have blown the gold in Vegas years ago.

(Dave Brennan)

Relationships should come with those little black
boxes that airplanes have. That way, when they
crash and burn, we'd actually get some answers.

(Corrina Bunch)

I'll bet I know something
about the guy who said, "The brain
is the most important sex organ."

(Jim Rosenberg)

Never get between a female grizzly
and one of her young, particularly if he's
just told her that he intends to drop
out of college to focus on his band.

(Andy Ihnatko)

If fruits were people, I'll bet
pineapples would be real bastards.

(Mystic Seven)

If I'm ever trapped somewhere and
have to drink my own urine, it had
better be in a wine cellar, because
I'd have to be really drunk to do it.

(Bob Warner)

I bet if you were a coyote and you got your
foot caught in a steel trap and chewed the
wrong leg off, you'd really feel pretty stupid.

(Lee Entrekin)

They say Disneyland is the happiest place
on earth, but I think that a laughing-gas
factory would be pretty tough competition.

(Greg Pettit)

If there really is a pole at
the North Pole, I bet there's some dead
explorer guy with his tongue stuck to it.

(Bob Van Voris)

You know the movie you're watching
is a chick flick if you wake up
and your wife is crying.

(Rick Oie)

The Top 15 Signs You Drank Too Much This Weekend

15. You spent Sunday night in jail for tipping cows — with your Oldsmobile.

14. Although armed with fire extinguishers, friends stood at a safe distance as you blew out your birthday candles.

13. Thanks to you, Jack Daniel's stock is up 15 1/4 since Friday.

12. Boris Yeltsin called personally to ask you to slow down on the Stoli.

11. For some reason, there's salt on the rim of your basketball goal.

10. Your name is Otis and Sheriff Andy has brought you some of Aunt Bea's pancakes.

9. For the money you spent on Thunderbird, you could've bought the *car*.

8. You're now the proud inventor of the "Slim Jim": Ultra Slim-Fast shakes made with Jim Beam.

7. Answering machine full of warnings from Coach Switzer.

6. Absolut wants to run an ad featuring a picture of your liver in the shape of a bottle.

5. Yet again, dry cleaner employees greet you with, "Hey, it's Vomit Man!"

4. The doorman asks for you ID just to see how long it'll take you to find your pants.

3. Your liver, in a fit of pique, leaps out of your abdominal cavity into a pan of frying onions.

2. Worried friends call Monday morning to make sure you returned the goat.

1. You're now sober enough to realize "Drink Canada Dry" is a slogan and not a personal challenge.

The list on the preceding page is from June 2, 1997.
It was compiled from 137 submissions from 47 contributors.

Martell Stroup, Reno, NV	– 1
Phil Doyle, Mercer Island, WA	– 2, Topic
Lev L. Spiro, Los Angeles, CA	– 3
Paul Lara, Temple, TX	– 4
Paul Schindler, Orinda, CA	– 5
Beth Kohl, Chicago, IL	– 6
George Olson, Colorado Springs, CO	– 7
Keith Martin, Atlanta, GA	– 8
Chris White, New York, NY	– 8
Jim Key, Garland, TX	– 9
Gene/Cynthia Markins-Dieden, New Haven, CT	– 10
Randy Wohl, Ma'ale Adumim, Israel	– 10
Marsha Clodfelter, Corpus Christi, TX	– 11
Jennifer Bieneman, Grand Rapids, MI	– 12
Jennifer Ritzinger, Seattle, WA	– 13
John Hering, Alexandria, VA	– 14
David G. Scott, Kansas City, MO	– 15

One day, I'm going to break Neil Armstrong's
record. Then *I'll* be the first man
to walk on the moon, and everyone will
forget all about that other first guy.

(Phil Jenkins)

On stormy days, I like to snuggle with my
girlfriend on the bearskin rug by the fireplace
with a bottle of really expensive sherry. But
only if my neighbor's out of town for the weekend,
'cause he's kind of touchy about his stuff.

(Tidewater Joe)

The Top 15 Questions on the
Spice Girl Job Application

15. In space provided, tell us why you want, why you really, really, want this job.

14. Do you have any detectable vestige of talent besides those hooters?

13. Would it, like, bother you to be the target of unrelenting hatred?

12. How would you best describe yourself?
    - ( ) an energetic self-starter
    - ( ) a team player
    - ( ) a tasty, albeit untalented, bit of crumpet

11. True or false: A mosh pit is the seed of the mosh fruit.

10. "I am willing to trade sexual favors for a career in the music industry."
    - ( ) yes   ( ) maybe

9. How many times have you been kicked out of a karaoke bar?

8. Does nudity bother you? If so, should I put my clothes back on?

7. Explain the difficulties in identifying the source of individual free will in light of the deterministic theories of neurochemical medicine and modern behavioralist psychology.
   Just kidding! Seriously, do you like leather mini-skirts?

6. Are you deceptively attractive in colored or stroboscopic light?

5. Choose an appropriate nickname:
   - ( ) Sexy   ( ) Nasty
   - ( ) Sweetie   ( ) Chlamydia

4. Have you ever been convicted of combining vertical and horizontal stripes?

3. If two trains leave Liverpool an hour apart at 90 kilometers, and 75 kilometers an hour, respectively, how would you look in spandex?

2. Does the term *force majeure in perpetuity* scare you or just make you giggly?

1. If required as part of your deal with Satan, would you be willing to help alleviate Prince Charles's loneliness?

The list on the preceding page is from June 11, 1997.
It was compiled from 78 submissions from 30 contributors.

Jonathan D. Colan, Miami, FL	– 1, 7
Martell Stroup, Reno, NV	– 2
David W. James, Los Angeles, CA	– 3
Dave George, Arlington, VA	– 4
Jeff Downey, Raleigh, NC	– 5, 15
Matt Loiselle, Detroit, MI	– 6
Chuck Smith, Woodbridge, VA	– 8
Paul Paternoster, Redwood City, CA	– 9
Bill Muse, Seattle, WA	– 10
Lev L. Spiro, Los Angeles, CA	– 10
R.M. Weiner, Brighton, MA	– 10
Glenn Marcus, Washington, DC	– 11
Lloyd Jacobson, Washington, DC	– 12, 15
LeMel Hebert-Williams, San Fran., CA	– 12, Topic
Phil Doyle, Mercer Island, WA	– 13
Alexander Clemens, San Fran, CA	– 14
Matt Alford, Portland, OR	– 15
Ed Smith, Chattanooga, TN	– 15

I think it would be fun if someone climbed
atop a city bus and pretended to be surfing.
It probably shouldn't be me, though,
'cause I fell off the first two times.

(LeMel Hebert-Williams)

Woo-hoo! I can say "I will not be obsessive
or compulsive" using 137 different voices
in reverse alphabetical order.

(Peter Casper)

The Top 15 Signs You're Too Old to Still Be a Virgin

15. You've resorted to cruising AARP meetings.

14. Impressed by your streak, Cal Ripken sends *you* fan letters.

13. Your home state? Arkansas. Your age? 12.

12. When you slip into something more comfortable, it's usually a coma.

11. Every night at home, your mother reminds you that all the other Supreme Court justices have had sex.

10. Black lace garter belt now attaches to your Depends.

9. Dating criteria have fallen from "rich and attractive" to "breathing."

8. The only tongue action you have enough energy for is to pop those dentures back into place.

7. When your date suggests you "get nasty," you start picking your nose.

6. You're the King of Pop, for crying out loud.

5. When ogling the pool boy, you usually covet his comfortable-looking sandals.

4. Mind addled by lack of sex, you find yourself standing at the altar next to John Tesh.

3. "Going all the way" takes on a whole new meaning, thanks to Metamucil.

2. Saving yourself for Ringo seemed like a groovy idea at the time.

1. Last young man you smiled at seductively escorted you across the street.

The list on the preceding page is from July 3, 1997.
It was compiled from 135 submissions from 47 contributors.

Caroline Gennity, Virginia Beach, VA	– 1
Jennifer O. Gall, Los Angeles, CA	– 2
Patrick Kachurek, Ann Arbor, MI	– 3
Craig Stacey, Lisle, IL	– 4
Cathie Walker, Victoria, BC, Canada	– 5
George Olson, Colorado Springs, CO	– 6
Bo Williams, Huntsville, AL	– 7
Steve Maybo, Carlsbad, CA	– 8
Dee Anne Phillips, Shreveport, LA	– 9
Doug Johnson, Santa Cruz, CA	– 10
Jonathan D. Colan, Miami, FL	– 11, 15
Beth Kohl, Chicago, IL	– 12
R.M. Weiner, Brighton, MA	– 13
Sue Prifogle, Rushville, IN	– 14
Tony Hill, Minneapolis, MN	– Topic

The thing I like about fantasy
is that I can afford it.

(Tom Sims)

How much joy could there have been in the
first place in a town named "Mudville"?

(Lev L. Spiro)

Every so often, I try to masturbate
a large word into conversation, even
if I'm not really sure what it means.

(Glenn Rauch)

The Top 15 Signs Your Librarian Is Nuts

15. Entire library stock replaced by 50,000 copies of *Yes, I Can* by Sammy Davis, Jr.

14. Half-dozen recently extracted tongues stapled to the "Quiet Please!" sign.

13. Recommends Kato Kaelin's book.

12. Instead of scanning barcode on book at checkout, seductively licks the inside cover.

11. Library only has two sections: "Limbaugh" and "Liddy."

10. Inserts boudoir photos of herself in copies of *Gray's Anatomy*.

9. When you ask for an appendix, she winks suggestively and shows you her scar.

8. Replaces the overdue-book fine with canings from the Rod of Literary Tardiness.

7. Files Art Buchwald under "Humor."

6. Always doing doughnuts with the bookmobile in the video store parking lot.

5. No matter what book you ask for, she hands you a piece of toast and a Q-Tip.

4. Uses the Dewar's Decimal System, which involves regular belts of Scotch.

3. Instead of a simple "Shhhh," uses a bullhorn to say, "One more sound and I cap yo' ass!"

2. Flashes patrons and yells, "Hey! Check *this* out!"

1. Leans over to whisper something and bites off half of your right ear.

The list on the preceding page is from July 16, 1997.
It was compiled from 119 submissions from 41 contributors.

John Hering, Alexandria, VA	– 1
Martell Stroup, Reno, NV	– 2
Bill Muse, Seattle, WA	– 3, 6
Randy Wohl, Ma'ale Adumim, Israel	– 3
Bruce Ansley, Baltimore, MD	– 4
R.M. Weiner, Brighton, MA	– 5
Chuck Smith, Woodbridge, VA	– 7
Jennifer Ritzinger, Seattle, WA	– 8, Topic
Kevin Hawley, Fairless Hills, PA	– 8
Marsha Clodfelter, Corpus Christi, TX	– 9
Lloyd Jacobson, Washington, DC	– 10
Matt Alford, Portland, OR	– 11
Bo Williams, Huntsville, AL	– 12
Tony Hill, Minneapolis, MN	– 13
Mark Schmidt, Santa Cruz, CA	– 14
Matt Loiselle, Detroit, MI	– 15
Paul Paternoster, Redwood City, CA	– Topic

I bet the reason chipmunks are always darting back and forth in utter fear is because they're afraid of being mistaken for that one chipmunk who slept with the preacher chipmunk's virgin daughter and robbed the chipmunk bank. 'Cause, dude, they all look the same.

(Amber Martinelli)

Time travel is great. I just wish we could get past that "one second forward" barrier.

(Josh Murtack)

The Top 15 Signs
Arnold Schwarzenegger Is 50 Years Old

15. His Humvee's left-turn signal is always on.

14. Varicose veins bulging out of his neck.

13. Black leather jacket and motorcycle boots replaced by taupe windbreaker and white loafers.

12. Can no longer throw Uncle Ted out of parties with one arm.

11. Maria falls asleep before he can get his broadsword ready, if you know what I mean.

10. Filming constantly interrupted with, "I'll be... *line, please!*"

9. Mr. Universe competition declines his suggestion for a "Best Gums Over 50" category.

8. Hemorrhoids now larger than biceps.

7. Concludes every failed bowel movement attempt by saying, "I'll be back."

6. Ever-increasing body count in *Grumpy Old Men* sequels since he joined the cast.

5. Has to stop and rest mid–last name when signing autographs.

4. Changed his name to Arnie Schwartz and moved to Miami to play bridge every Tuesday and Friday afternoon.

3. Most explosions in latest flick are the result of his worsening lactose intolerance.

2. Every plot: Get revenge upon neighborhood kids for walking on his lawn.

1. Has begun tucking his pecs into the front of his pants.

The list on the preceding page is from August 5, 1997.
It was compiled from 98 submissions from 38 contributors.

John Voigt, Chicago, IL	– 1
Bill Muse, Seattle, WA	– 2, 3
David W. James, Los Angeles, CA	– 2
Eric Huret, Atlanta, GA	– 4, 7
Martell Stroup, Reno, NV	– 5
Keith Martin, Atlanta, GA	– 6
Dennis Koho, Keizer, OR	– 8
Lev L. Spiro, Los Angeles, CA	– 9
Wade Kwon, Birmingham, AL	– 10, 15
Matt Diamond, Holland, PA	– 10
Sue Prifogle, Rushville, IN	– 11
Joel McClure, Royal Oak, MI	– 12
Cathie Walker, Victoria, BC, Canada	– 13
Paul Paternoster, Redwood City, CA	– 14
Alexander Clemens, San Francisco, CA	– 15
Chris White, New York, NY	– Topic

You say "to-may-toe." I say "to-mah-toe."
You say, "Is it necessary to constantly correct me?"
I say, "It wouldn't be if you got it right."
You say, "I'm sleeping with your brother."
I say what sounds like blubbering.
Let's call the whole thing off.

(Jim Rosenberg)

You'll go through more hamsters than
you'd think before you finally come across
one that can make a decent cup of coffee.

(Andy Ihnatko)

The Top 15 Chinese Translations of English Movie Titles

15. *Pretty Woman — I Will Marry a Prostitute to Save Money*

14. *Face/Off — Who Is Face Belonging To? I Kill You Again, Harder!*

13. *Leaving Las Vegas — I'm Drunk and You're a Prostitute*

12. *Interview With the Vampire — So, You Are a Lawyer?*

11. *The Piano — Ungrateful Adulteress! I Chop Off Your Finger!*

10. *My Best Friend's Wedding — Help! My Pretend Boyfriend Is Gay!*

9. *George of the Jungle — Big Dumb Monkey-Man Keeps Whacking Tree With Genitals*

8. *Scent of a Woman — Great Buddha! I Can Smell You From Afar! Take a Bath, Will You?!*

7. *Love, Valour, Compassion! — I Am That Guy From Seinfeld So It's Acceptable for Straight People to Enjoy This Gay Movie*

6. *Babe — The Happy Dumpling-to-Be Who Talks and Solves Agricultural Problems*

5. *Twister — Run! Ruuunnnn! Cloudzillaaaaa!*

4. *Field of Dreams — Imaginary Dead Baseball Players Live in My Cornfield*

3. *Barb Wire — Delicate Orbs of Womanhood Bigger Than Your Head Can Hurt You*

2. *Batman & Robin — Come to My Cave and Wear This Rubber Codpiece, Cute Boy*

1. *The Crying Game — Oh No! My Girlfriend Has a Penis!*

The list on the preceding page is from August 25, 1997.
It was compiled from 96 submissions from 35 contributors.

Bill Muse, Seattle, WA	– 1, 11, 15
Sam Evans, Charleston, SC	– 2, 7
Gene Markins-Dieden, New Haven, CT	– 3
Kevin Hawley, Fairless Hills, PA	– 4
Caroline Gennity, VA	– 5, 8, 12
Jeff Scherer, Brooklyn, NY	– 6, 10, Topic
Lev L. Spiro, Los Angeles, CA	– 9, 14
Fred Hesby, Portland, OR	– 13

You know, I just can't see
the mother of the guy who invented
suppositories bragging about it.

(Anna L. Juarez)

There are some things from
the past that come back to haunt you.
And I bet an ex-wife with a
meat cleaver is one of them.

(Don Swain)

I think a really funny joke would be for
NASA to send up rockets and push a bunch
of planets out of alignment. Then they could
sit back and laugh when everyone realizes
that their horoscopes aren't coming true.

(Davejames)

The Top 15 Bad Romance Novel Opening Lines (Part I)

15. "He snapped my bra like a Concorde taking off, and I was unhooked for love."

14. "Yes, she was a woman who had once been a man, but she still knew how to flutter her eyelashes as well as those other hussies."

13. "The heaving waves on the vast, ink-black ocean sent a salty spray over the proud bow of the three-masted ship, leaving beads of water on the exposed alabaster skin above the bodice of the tall, raven-haired woman who stood sobbing on the deck, her salty tears mixing with the storm-tossed sea."

12. "Scarlett's hair was as red as my persistent canker sore."

11. "Nicolette let the silk blouse fall from her shoulders, wrapped her left leg around John and deftly cut some cheese."

10. "Robert was new at this prison thing, and he felt frightened and confused. But the moment he laid eyes on #472825994, he became a prisoner of love."

9. "Sam liked to hump."

8. "Though flanked by two swarthy state troopers, Paula found her gaze drawn to the chubby saxophonist."

7. "It was a dark and horny night."

6. "Gentle cascades of vermilion poured over Daphne's heaving, lily-white bosom. 'Call 911, Scooby,' she breathed."

5. "His flatulence reared up like a proud stallion."

4. "'Miss Savannah, is there room for both of us in that hoop skirt?' Chandler mocked with a slight bow and a sweep of his top hat."

3. "Within minutes of their meeting, Representatives Beth (D-Florida) and Eric (R-Montana) lumbered into the bedroom, where soon the unmistakable sounds of wet, naked bodies engaged in a sexual congress were heard."

2. "He smelled of pork. Rotting pork, in fact, and lots of it."

1. "Omaha Beach, 0800 hours: Reinforcements from 2nd Panzer Korps arrive, their well-muscled young torsos glistening with man-dew."

The list on the preceding page is from August 29, 1997. It was compiled from 104 submissions from 41 contributors.

Lev L. Spiro, Los Angeles, CA	– 1, Topic
Steve Hurd, San Ramon, CA	– 2
Dennis Koho, Keizer, OR	– 3
Marsha Clodfelter, Corpus Christi, TX	– 4
Paul Paternoster, Redwood City, CA	– 5
Michael Wolf, Brookline, MA	– 6
Sue Prifogle, Rushville, IN	– 7
Barbara Rush, Tulsa, OK	– 8
Beth Kohl, Chicago, IL	– 9
Rob Seulowitz, New York, NY	– 10
Ed Smith, Chattanooga, TN	– 10
Dave Henry, Slidell, LA	– 11
Jim Rosenberg, Greensboro, NC	– 12
Phil Doyle, Mercer Island, WA	– 13
Jennifer Bieneman, Grand Rapids, MI	– 14
Ed Brooksbank, Sacramento, CA	– 15

I can see now, months later, that breaking up
with my ex-girlfriend was the best thing for
me, as it allowed me to go out and do those
things that she always prevented me
from doing — like her really hot friend.

(Mike Iaia)

If you fall from the top of a skyscraper,
only scream when passing open windows,
because the closed windows are usually soundproof
and hey, you'd just be wasting your breath.

(R.M. Weiner)

The Top 15 Bad Romance Novel Opening Lines (Part II)

15. "Hers was a dark and stormy loin."

14. "The T. rex stopped to stare at the female, its tawny pecs rippling in the dappled light."

13. "Her eyes were a beautiful bright blue. Her lips full and sensual. And her legs strong and firm, all four of them."

12. "Nick Adams held the corset in his hand. It was a good corset. It would rip when he ripped it. Nick liked that."

11. "Her habit clung to her body like leather to a bible."

10. "Her voice quivered like a plate of Jell-O on a fault line, and her body was soon to follow."

9. "Flinging her abusive husband's genitalia out the car window, Lorena felt a long-overdue sense of freedom."

8. "Long auburn hair flowing out behind her, dress billowing in the breeze, Cassandra had given in to gravity's pull and hit the pavement like a bag of fresh phlegm."

7. "I couldn't take my eyes off of his rippling physique, his dark leonine mane, his sensual lips, and his skim, no foam, double cappuccino, half-caf, half-decaf eyes."

6. "The very sight of him made me forget Paris and long for New Jersey."

5. "With great trepidation, Richard Jewell walked the six flights of stairs to the apartment he shared with his mother."

4. "Her bosom was heaving uncontrollably; she doubted she'd make it to the toilet on time."

3. "I blushed as the captain strode toward me in his manly way, took me in his arms and whispered, 'Make it so, Number One! Engage!'"

2. "The man-probe dug in deep while NASA engineers gawked in lecherous pleasure."

1. "Marv Albert strutted into the Ritz with a twinkle in his eye and a gleam in his incisors."

The list on the preceding page is from September 3, 1997. It was compiled from 104 submissions from 41 contributors.

Fred Hesby, Portland, OR	– 1
Matt Alford, Portland, OR	– 2
Rob Seulowitz, New York, NY	– 3, 12
Peg Warner, Derry, NH	– 4
Jim Rosenberg, Greensboro, NC	– 5
Steve Hurd, San Ramon, CA	– 6
Gene Markins-Dieden, New Haven, CT	– 7
Caroline Gennity, Virginia Beach, VA	– 8
Matt Diamond, Holland, PA	– 9
Jonathan D. Colan, Miami, FL	– 10
Beth Kohl, Chicago, IL	– 11
R.M. Weiner, Brighton, MA	– 13
Lev L. Spiro, Los Angeles, CA	– 14, Topic
Bill Muse, Seattle, WA	– 15

I bet really good magicians always
leave church with a little more
money than they came in with.

(Andy Pierson)

Oh, what a tangled web we weave
when we don't shave our legs for four
weeks and then stuff them into pantyhose.

(Elizabeth McLeod)

As I walk through the valley of the shadow
of death, I shall fear no ev— Hey! A penny!

(Caleb Ronsen)

The Top 15 Signs Your Local Girl Scout Troop Hates You

15. *Your* box of Samoa cookies reads: MADE WITH REAL SAMOANS.

14. DIE, YUPPIE SCUM! spelled out in Thin Mints across your driveway.

13. That burning fleur-de-lis on your lawn.

12. You've never heard of a Peanut Butter With Glass Shards-flavor cookie.

11. New oath: "A Girl Scout is courteous and kind to everyone, except for Bob Smith."

10. Your picture is next to the "Bad Touching" section of the training materials.

9. Troop meetings always end with a rousing game of "Kick Bob's Ass."

8. The cookies in your box have enough needles in them to start your own sweatshop.

7. Instead of helping you cross the street, they just give you a swift kick in the ass and push you into traffic.

6. Your box of Thin Mints comes with all the chocolate licked off.

5. When passing by your house, they flip you off and shout, "Kumbaya *this!*"

4. Every Scout on your block has earned her Egg Bob Smith's House merit badge.

3. For their Animal Behavior merit badge, they spay your dog.

2. You wake up to find a My Little Pony head in your bed.

1. Burning macrame bag of Rover's excretions left on your doorstep.

The list on the preceding page is from September 10, 1997. It was compiled from 108 submissions from 44 contributors.

Chuck Smith, Woodbridge, VA	– 1
Gail Celio, Athens, GA	– 1, 15
Bill Gray, Waterloo, ON, Canada	– 2
Lev L. Spiro, Los Angeles, CA	– 3
Eric Huret, Atlanta, GA	– 4
John Voigt, Chicago, IL	– 4
R.M. Weiner, Brighton, MA	– 4
Cathie Walker, Victoria, BC, Canada	– 5, 7
Wade Kwon, Birmingham, AL	– 6
Caroline Gennity, Virginia Beach, VA	– 7
Dave Wesley, Pleasant Hill, CA	– 7
Martell Stroup, Reno, NV	– 8
David Hyatt, New York, NY	– 9
Jim Rosenberg, Greensboro, NC	– 10
Geoff Brown, Farmington Hills, MI	– 11
Kris Johnson, Burbank, CA	– 12
Sue Prifogle, Rushville, IN	– 13
Jeff Scherer, Brooklyn, NY	– 14
Jennifer Ritzinger, Seattle, WA	– Topic

My boss says I have to take cultural sensitivity classes. Whatever. I just hope the teacher ain't some stupid foreigner.

(Mark Niebuhr)

It's not true that the sun always sets in the west — I went to New York last month and it set there, too.

(Denny Silverman)

I think someone should invent
Beergard, because how often do you
actually spill Scotch on the carpet?

(Chris Sampson)

Sometimes I'll think, "Is life worth living?"
and then I'll think, "Is death worth dying?"
and then I'll think, "Is cheese worth cheesing?"
and then I'll think, "Whew! I've had enough to drink!"

(R.M. Weiner)

Give a man a fish and he eats for a day,
but give a screaming baby a bottle of
Drano and suddenly I'm the bad guy!

(Lynn Pruett)

I think in a past life I was a ruler in Egypt.
I can tell because I really like wearing sandals.

(Tom Sims)

If life gives you lemons, ask for a receipt,
because if life is just giving stuff away
willy-nilly like that, there's a pretty good
chance it's just unloading stolen goods.

(Davejames)

If you're ever in a really fancy restaurant
and they have a menu item called "Naughty,
Spanked Lobster," I say get it, because with
those swanky places, you never know.

(Mark Niebuhr)

At first I thought, "How could women be from
Venus? It's got an atmosphere of poisonous gas!"
And then I made the connection: potpourri!

(Larry Hollister)

If I can make just one person laugh,
then it must've been a pretty good eulogy.

(Wade Kwon)

Some days make you wonder if you've
made bad choices in your life.
Especially those days when the FBI
shows up and digs in your back yard.

(Bob Van Voris)

To everything, turn, turn, turn.
There is a season, turn, turn, turn.
Then fall on your dizzy ass, bright guy.

(Doug Finney)

The Top 16 Signs You've Chosen the Wrong Mount Everest Guide

16. The last three days, all you've had to eat is s'mores.

15. Every morning, greets the group with, "Wonder who'll die today?"

14. Doesn't worry about provisions, as there's bound to be a Starbucks or McDonald's every half mile or so.

13. Gets lost in the "Sherpa Shack" gift shop.

12. Makes everyone do upside-down shots from the St. Bernard's collar.

11. First day's preparation devoted entirely to making snow angels.

10. Every 10 minutes, stops and yells, "*Ricola!*"

9. Throws a fit when her stiletto heel gets stuck in the ice.

8. Has everyone stick their tongues to a cherry Popsicle "for practice."

7. Keeps repeating, "Is it me, or is it cold up here?"

6. "Map, schmap — you can see the top from here!"

5. Two words: golf clubs

4. Forgets to wear socks with his sandals.

3. Keeps using the oxygen tanks to make balloon animals.

2. Every so often, turns and screams, "Stop following me!"

1. Squeezes your ass, then yells, "Hey, if we get stranded we can live off Tubby here for a week!"

The list on the preceding page is from September 16, 1997.
It was compiled from 113 submissions from 43 contributors.

Ed Brooksbank, Sacramento, CA	– 1
Caroline Gennity, Virginia Beach, VA	– 2
Jason Anderson, Birmingham, AL	– 3
Joel McClure, Royal Oak, MI	– 4, 14
Lev L. Spiro, Los Angeles, CA	– 5
Jennifer Bieneman, Grand Rapids, MI	– 6
David G. Scott, Kansas City, MO	– 7, 16
Marsha Clodfelter, Corpus Christi, TX	– 8, Topic
Sue Prifogle, Rushville, IN	– 9
Sam Evans, Charleston, SC	– 10, 15
Kim Moser, New York, NY	– 11
Beth Kohl, Chicago, IL	– 12
Denis Rubin, Los Angeles, CA	– 13
Steve Hurd, San Ramon, CA	– 14

What you know is not as important as
who you know. But what you know about
who you know is where the *real* money is.

(Slick Sharkey)

It was looking pretty hopeless for getting
a second date until she bailed me out
with that "over my dead body" clause.

(Joseph Moore)

As far as ineffectual suicide methods go,
I'm sticking with Visine.

(Christy Simuangco)

The Top 16 Signs Your Cat
Is Plotting World Domination

16. Sits on your newspaper in the morning and carefully reads the coded message that Garfield sends out every day.

15. Used to sleep on top of TV, now monitors CNN 24 hours a day.

14. Notably absent from home during surprise feline invasion of Poland.

13. When you enter the room, Snowball and the other members of the Tri-Cateral Commission stop talking and begin playing with yarn.

12. Behind the couch you find a forged passport, plane tickets and nine suicide bombs.

11. What you thought was "heat" is actually a four-legged goose step.

10. Well, *somebody* subscribed to alt.cats.world.domination.

9. Autopsy of the last mouse left on your doormat reveals "tattoo" to be blueprint of the U.N. building.

8. Constantly petting that bald man he keeps on his lap.

7. Kitty Chow spilled on the floor spells out "Drop the car keys and leave the door open or the dog gets it in the head."

6. Then: dead mice in the kitchen.
   Now: dead Third World dictators in the basement.

5. Judging from the kitchen, he seems to be working on some kind of "land mine" technology.

4. Fluffy is now sleeping only 21 hours a day, down from 23.

3. Has recently been acting somewhat... aloof.

2. What your cat lacks in charisma and good looks, he makes up for with his ruthless handling of rival software companies.

1. Somehow, you're now subscribed to *Pussy of Fortune* magazine.

The list on the preceding page is from October 10, 1997. It was compiled from 128 submissions from 47 contributors.

Jim Rosenberg, Greensboro, NC	– 1, 10
Don Swain, Pontiac, MI	– 2
Lev L. Spiro, Los Angeles, CA	– 3, 9
Alexander Clemens, San Francisco, CA	– 4, 7
Gayle Ehrenman, New York, NY	– 4
Paul Paternoster, Redwood City, CA	– 4
John Voigt, Chicago, IL	– 5
David W. James, Los Angeles, CA	– 6, 11
Tom Louderback, Boston, MA	– 6
Matt Diamond, Holland, PA	– 8
Bill Muse, Seattle, WA	– 12
Larry Baum, Hong Kong	– 13
George Olson, Colorado Springs, CO	– 13
Tisha Stacey, Lisle, IL	– 14, Topic
Josh Robertson, Bronx, NY	– 15
Dave Henry, Slidell, LA	– 16

After the meek inherit the earth,
we should just kick their
butts and take it from them.

(Jim Rosenberg)

I think it would be kind of cool if tortillas were called "Mohicans" instead. That way, if there were only one left, I could ask, "Does anyone mind if I grabbed the last of the Mohicans?" and everybody would laugh. If I actually liked tortillas, that is.

(Pang E. Sass)

The Top 16 Most Ironic Celebrity Deaths

16. Charlton Heston — shot by an ape cleaning its semi-automatic "hunting rifle"

15. Pamela Anderson Lee — boobytrap

14. Susan Lucci — tripped and broke her neck while running up steps to accept Emmy

13. Barry White — ambushed by a squad of confused Girl Scout leaders

12. Alanis Morissette — killed just after winning the lottery at age 98, in a car accident during a traffic jam on her own rainy wedding day while receiving a prepaid free ride from three women who look just like her but with worse hair

11. Anna Nicole Smith — suffocated while working out on a slant board

10. Jenny McCarthy — struck by a random thought

9. Marlon Brando — choked to death while eating buttered popcorn at 25th-anniversary screening of *Last Tango in Paris*

8. Keith Richards — natural causes

7. RuPaul — prostate cancer

6. Madonna — exposure

5. Al Gore — Dutch Elm disease

4. Keanu Reeves — brain tumor

3. Marv Albert — hit by Victoria's Secret delivery truck outside Carpet World

2. Pee Wee Herman — died by his own hand

1. Gallagher — killed by Smashing Pumpkins

The list on the preceding page is from October 17, 1997. It was compiled from 146 submissions from 54 contributors.

Peter Bauer, Rochester, NY	– 1
Chuck Smith, Woodbridge, VA	– 2, 6, 7
Barbara McMahon, Ann Arbor, MI	– 3
Caroline Gennity, Virginia Beach, VA	– 4, 15
David W. James, Los Angeles, CA	– 5, Topic
Jonathan D. Colan, Miami, FL	– 8
Kevin Hawley, Fairless Hills, PA	– 8
Glenn Marcus, Washington, DC	– 9
Rob Seulowitz, New York, NY	– 10
Vickie Neilson, Carlsbad, CA	– 11
Josh Robertson, Bronx, NY	– 12
Don Swain, Pontiac, MI	– 13
Jennifer O. Gall, Los Angeles, CA	– 14
Christopher Troise, New York, NY	– 14
Sue Prifogle, Rushville, IN	– 16

Even though I've achieved a modest amount of
financial success in my life, which has allowed
me to move into better and better neighborhoods,
I now realize that all I'm doing is getting
nicer and nicer places in which to masturbate.

(Bill Grieser)

Since computers basically just use ones and zeroes,
someone should invent a binary keyboard —
one with just two really big keys on it.
The cool thing about it would be that you
could type on it with your butt cheeks.

(Whil Hentzen)

The Top 15 Freudian Pick-Up Lines

15. "My sign is Ramses, what's yours?"

14. "You're one hot mama... but of course, all women are!"

13. "You ego may be saying 'no,' but your id is giving me a tongue bath."

12. "Wanna come back to my place and do something you'll repress later?"

11. "Did I tell you I'm a certified pubic accountant?"

10. "Y'know, a few minutes of probing on my couch and you'd be a completely different woman."

9. "You *must* be tired, because you've been running through my passive-aggressive, libido-suppressed mind all night."

8. "You remind me of my mother when she was Jung."

7. "Excuse me, but I couldn't help noticing that you're also putting hot dogs through doughnuts."

6. "I'll envy yours, if you'll envy mine."

5. "Mind if I put my cigar in your ashtray?"

4. "I believe in putting the 'psycho' back in 'psychoanalysis.'"

3. "Can I buy you a shrink?"

2. "Oops! I mean *Horatio*! My name is Horatio."

1. "... and ven I snap my fingers, you vill put your clothes back on and remember none of zis."

The list on the preceding page is from October 27, 1997.
It was compiled from 97 submissions from 38 contributors.

Don Swain, Pontiac, MI	– 1, Topic
Larry Baum, Hong Kong	– 2
Denis Rubin, Los Angeles, CA	– 3, 8
Wade Kwon, Birmingham, AL	– 4
Bill Muse, Seattle, WA	– 5
Bruce Ansley, Baltimore, MD	– 6, 13
Peter Bauer, Rochester, NY	– 7
David G. Scott, Kansas City, MO	– 9
Steve Hurd, San Ramon, CA	– 10, 14
Jennifer Ritzinger, Seattle, WA	– 10
Jim Rosenberg, Greensboro, NC	– 11
Jonathan D. Colan, Miami, FL	– 12
Paul Schindler, Orinda, CA	– 15

If life is but a dream, then
where's my underwear-model husband?

(Joy Wallace)

I wonder if topless dancers
ever get pulled over on their way
to work for driving erotically?

(Wiley)

A woman uses thousands of facial tissues a year.
A careful man, however, can use one handkerchief
for about eight months before it gets full.

(Michael Cunningham)

The Top 15 19th-Century Euphemisms for Masturbation

16. Emptyin' the Saloon

15. Pocket Punch 'n' Judy

14. Signing Your John Hancock

13. Dragging Thyself to Hell, One Hand's Breadth at a Time

12. Waving to Queen Victoria

11. Trying for a Scarlet "M"

10. Oiling the Pennywhistle

9. Assaulting the Tower of London

8. Cleaning the Musket

7. Quashing the Southern Uprising

6. Monitoring Your Merrimac

5. Driving the Golden Spike

4. Delivering the Ejaculation Proclamation

3. Churning the Codpiece Butter

2. Square Dancing With Satan

1. Addressing Lord Palmer

The list on the preceding page is from November 4, 1997. It was compiled from 117 submissions from 43 contributors.

Lev L. Spiro, Los Angeles, CA	– 1
Mitch Patterson, Atlanta, GA	– 2
Bill Muse, Seattle, WA	– 3, 8, Topic
Bruce Ansley, Baltimore, MD	– 3
Matt Loiselle, Detroit, MI	– 3
Bo Williams, Huntsville, AL	– 3
Dave Wesley, Pleasant Hill, CA	– 4
Steve Hurd, San Ramon, CA	– 5
David W. James, Los Angeles, CA	– 6, 8
Patrick Douglas Crispen, U. of Alabama	– 7
Natasha Filipovic, New York, NY	– 8
Brad Schreiber, Los Angeles, CA	– 9
Kim Moser, New York, NY	– 10
R.M. Weiner, Somerville, MA	– 11
Sue Prifogle, Rushville, IN	– 12, 16
Blair Bostick, Alexandria, VA	– 12
Ed Brooksbank, Sacramento, CA	– 12
Kevin Hawley, Fairless Hills, PA	– 12
Christopher Troise, New York, NY	– 13
Troy Roberson, Birmingham, AL	– 14
Jeff Scherer, Brooklyn, NY	– 15

My doctor just said I have something called "natural causes." Should I be worried?

(Bob Van Voris)

If we are to learn anything of value from *Star Trek*, it's that the universe is filled with vastly different styles of foreheads.

(Chris Needles)

The Top 16 Signs Your Date's Not an English Major

16. She thinks Jack London is a character on *General Hospital*.

15. Has legally changed her name to Slutty Spice.

14. Won't stop talking about the time he bit Holyfield's ear.

13. Wants to buy the novel of the Mr. Bean movie.

12. The two of you constantly argue about which Homer came first.

11. Giggles uncontrollably whenever you bring up *Moby-Dick*.

10. Thinks *Elements of Style* was written by Elsa Klensch.

9. The last time he completed a sentence, he was at Attica.

8. "You gots no condom, you gets no party" was your last clue.

7. "Of *course* I've read *Walden*. And it only took me 10 minutes to find him!"

6. Ask her to conjugate a verb and she starts talking and belching at the same time.

5. Doesn't have a lot of free weekends due to busy schedule as NASCAR commentator.

4. Thinks *Beowulf* is a show starring David Hasselhoff.

3. Her favorite poem deals with a man from Nantucket.

2. When you ask if he has any Grey Poupon, he says, "Hey, don't be gross!"

1. You: "Shall I compare thee to a summer's day?"
   Her: "Dude! That would be, like, totally bitchin'!"

The list on the preceding page is from November 11, 1997. It was compiled from 115 submissions from 43 contributors.

Jonathan D. Colan, Miami, FL	– 1
Marshal Perlman, Minneapolis, MN	– 2
David G. Scott, Kansas City, MO	– 3, 10
Peter Bauer, Rochester, NY	– 4, 11
Lev L. Spiro, Los Angeles, CA	– 4
Jeff Downey, Raleigh, NC	– 5
Sam Evans, Charleston, SC	– 6
Troy Roberson, Birmingham, AL	– 7
Ed Brooksbank, Sacramento, CA	– 8
Denis Rubin, Los Angeles, CA	– 9
Paul Paternoster, Redwood City, CA	– 11
Martell Stroup, Reno, NV	– 11
Kevin Freels, Sun Valley, CA	– 12
John Voigt, Chicago, IL	– 13, 15
Bill Muse, Seattle, WA	– 14
Dave Wesley, Pleasant Hill, CA	– 16
Don Swain, Pontiac, MI	– Topic

Give a man a fish and he'll eat for a day.
Teach a man to fish and he'll eat for a lifetime.
Get a man hammered on Jagermeister at the company holiday party and you can talk him into eating tropical fish from the reception room aquarium.

(Chris White)

They say the three most important things in real estate are lubrication, lubrication and lubrication. On second thought, maybe I should have asked to see that guy's real estate license.

(Bob Van Voris)

The Top 16 MENSA Pick-Up Lines

16. "This is your brain. This is your brain on my naked thigh. Any questions?"

15. "Could you help me get this tie tack out of my hand?"

14. "Toward what end does a substantially empathetic demoiselle such as yourself inhabit a locus such as this?"

13. "What say we skip this nerd-fest and hit an all-night symposium on Euclidean geometry?"

12. "Perchance, would you be inclined to participate, at my domicile, sans apparel, in a modicum of copulation?"

11. "It doesn't take a genius to see how gorgeous you are, but if it did, I'd be overqualified."

10. "You'll have to excuse me — your presence excites me beyond all capacity for cognitive discourse."

9. "Veni, vidi, va-va-voom!"

8. "You must be tired, because you've been running quadratic equations through my mind all night."

7. "That tape on your glasses really sets off your eyes."

6. "According to Heisenberg's Uncertainty Principle of quantum mechanics, we may already be making love right now."

5. "If I were to mention to you that you have a bellus corpus, would you take umbrage?"

4. "I bet your brain stem reaches almost down to your gluteus maximus."

3. "Ooohh, your IQ is 145? I like 'em dumb and strong!"

2. "By visually measuring the wrinkles in the front of your pants, calculating your body mass based on your height and weight, and dividing that number by your waist size, I conclude that you have absolutely nothing in your pocket and are, in fact, glad to see me."

1. "Baby, I'll have you barking like a *canis familiaris*."

The list on the preceding page is from December 4, 1997.
It was compiled from 176 submissions from 65 contributors.

Peter Bauer, Rochester, NY	– 1, 3, 12
Eric Huret, Atlanta, GA	– 2
Sue Prifogle, Rushville, IN	– 4
Randy Wohl, Ma'ale Adumim, Israel	– 5
Jonathan D. Colan, Miami, FL	– 6
William Gray, San Jose, CA	– 6
Bill Muse, Seattle, WA	– 7
Bob Mader, Knoxville, TN	– 8
David G. Scott, Kansas City, MO	– 8
Daniel Weckerly, Limerick, PA	– 9
Paul Paternoster, Redwood City, CA	– 10
Phil Doyle, Mercer Island, WA	– 11
Dave Henry, Slidell, LA	– 12
Mark Schmidt, Santa Cruz, CA	– 13
Lev L. Spiro, Los Angeles, CA	– 14, 16
Chuck Smith, Woodbridge, VA	– 15, Topic

I told my girlfriend last night how
much I loved her, and she said that
I must have been out drinking again.
I asked her why she would say that,
and she said, "Because I'm your father."

(Dave George)

As a graduation gift to myself, I bought
a really bad toupee. I figure that if I wear it
over my real hair all the time, by the time
I go bald in 30 years or so everyone will
figure it's just how my hair normally looks.

(Andy Ihnatko)

The Top 16 Fatal Things to Say to Your Pregnant Wife (Part I)

16. "Not to imply anything, but I don't think the kid weighs 40 pounds."

15. "Y'know, looking at her, you'd never guess that Pamela Lee had a baby!"

14. "I sure hope your thighs aren't gonna stay that flabby forever!"

13. "Well, couldn't they induce labor? The 25th is the Super Bowl."

12. "Damn if you ain't about five pounds away from a surprise visit from that Richard Simmons fella."

11. "Fred at the office passed a stone the size of a pea. Boy, that's gotta hurt."

10. "Whoa! For a minute there, I thought I woke up next to Willard Scott!"

9. "I'm jealous! Why can't men experience the joy of childbirth?"

8. "Are your ankles supposed to look like that?"

7. "Get your *own* ice cream, Buddha!"

6. "Geez, you're awfully puffy looking today."

5. "Got milk?"

4. "Maybe we should name the baby after my secretary, Tawney."

3. "Man! That rose tattoo on your hip is the size of Madagascar!"

2. "Retaining water? Yeah, like the Hoover Dam retains water."

1. "You don't have the guts to pull the trigger, Lardass."

The list on the preceding page is from December 11, 1997.
It was compiled from 143 submissions from 52 contributors.

R.M. Weiner, Somerville, MA	– 1
Paul Paternoster, Redwood City, CA	– 2
David G. Scott, Kansas City, MO	– 3
Don Swain, Pontiac, MI	– 4
Martell Stroup, Reno, NV	– 5, 7
Kermit Woodall, Richmond, VA	– 6
Cathie Walker, Victoria, BC, Canada	– 8
Jeff Scherer, Brooklyn, NY	– 9
Sue Prifogle, Rushville, IN	– 10
Eric Huret, Atlanta, GA	– 11
Caroline Gennity, Virginia Beach, VA	– 12
Peter Bauer, Rochester, NY	– 13
Yoram Puius, Bronx, NY	– 14
Kevin Freels, Sun Valley, CA	– 15, Topic
William Gray, San Jose, CA	– 16

Despite what the laws of physics dictate,
you can go faster than the car in front of you.
The problem is that you can only do it once.

(Debbie Ryan)

Not even Darth Vader is evil enough to
embrace the *paisley* side of the Force.

(James Knowles)

I bet a lot of mimes choke to death because
nobody believes they're really choking.

(John Gephart)

The Top 16 Fatal Things to Say to Your Pregnant Wife (Part II)

16. "Sure you'll get your figure back — we'll just search 1985, where you left it."

15. "Keys are on the fridge, honey. I'll see you at the hospital at halftime."

14. "Sure, the doctor said you're eating for two — but he didn't mean two orcas."

13. "Honey, come show the guys your Brando impression!"

12. "Roseanne, what have you done with my wife?!"

11. "How come you're so much fatter than the other chicks in Lamaze?"

10. "Sweetheart, where'd you put that Victoria's Secret catalog?"

9. "What's the big deal? If you can handle *me* going in, surely you can handle a baby coming out."

8. "Hey, when you're finished pukin' in there, get me a beer, willya?"

7. "Why in the *world* would I want to rub your feet?"

6. "That's not a bun in the oven — it's the whole friggin' bakery!"

5. "You know, now that you mention it, you *are* getting fat and unattractive."

4. "Oh, this is just great! Now, on top of everything else, child support."

3. "Yo, fatass! You're blocking the TV!"

2. "No, I don't know where the remote is! Have you looked under your breasts?"

1. "I know today's your due date, but Larry just got a 10-point buck and that's a reason to celebrate, too."

The list on the preceding page is from December 12, 1997.
It was compiled from 143 submissions from 52 contributors.

Jennifer Bieneman, Grand Rapids, MI	– 1
Caroline Gennity, Virginia Beach, VA	– 2
John Voigt, Chicago, IL	– 3
Don Swain, Pontiac, MI	– 4
Denis Rubin, Los Angeles, CA	– 5
Steve Hurd, San Ramon, CA	– 6
Kermit Woodall, Richmond, VA	– 7
Lev L. Spiro, Los Angeles, CA	– 8, 11
Barry T. Smith, Boulder Creek, CA	– 9
Jonathan D. Colan, Miami, FL	– 10
Alan Wagner, Bayside, WI	– 10
Dave Wesley, Pleasant Hill, CA	– 12
Peter Bauer, Rochester, NY	– 13
David G. Scott, Kansas City, MO	– 13
Annie Fisher, Philadelphia, PA	– 14
Geoff Brown, Farmington Hills, MI	– 15
William Gray, San Jose, CA	– 15
David W. James, Los Angeles, CA	– 16
Kevin Freels, Sun Valley, CA	– Topic

My wife is crazy with forgetfulness. I found
about a dozen condoms in her suitcase, so she
even forgot that I'm not coming on this trip!
What a not-remembering nut she is!

(Jim Rosenberg)

Sometimes after sex I want to take a nap,
but when I hang up the phone and realize how
much money I just spent, I'm not tired anymore.

(Derek Winsworth)

If I had a nickel for every paycheck I've
blown on cocaine and cheap hookers, I could
spend a whole weekend doing nothing but...
well, you probably see where this is headed.

(Chris White)

Life isn't fair. During her senior year
in high school, Britney Spears had a growth
spurt in her mammary area. In *my* senior
year, I had a growth spurt in my ass area.

(Neva R. Huddleston)

Between the time saved always using
the carpool lane and the hassle saved
never cleaning bird crap off of your car,
it's a wonder more people don't drive
with scarecrows in the passenger seat.

(Davejames)

If I ever had a talking
dog, I'd train it to say,
"Help! The dog ate me!
Get me outta here!"

(Mike McClaren)

I don't know if I'll ever discover
the meaning of life, but if some of the clues
are visible on the upper torsos of women
wearing halter tops, I like my odds.

(Tommy Jack)

As a parent, I believe in
the concept of tough love.
Yesterday, I finally had to say
to my child, *"Will you shut up
about the damn Care Bears?!"*

(Jim Rosenberg)

I think NASCAR would be much more
exciting if, like in a skating rink,
every 15 minutes someone announced
it was time to reverse direction.

(Jeffrey Anbinder)

I told the teacher that my son wasn't very
smart, and she said something about the acorn not
falling far from the tree. Since I never studied
treeology, I don't have a clue what that means.

(Michael Cunningham)

The Top 17 Pet Peeves of James Bond

17. Tomorrow never dies... and neither does this blasted cold sore.

16. Despite knighting by the queen, still can't get a date with Baby Spice.

15. Getting harder and harder to use his nuclear-powered-heat-seeking-homing-device-in-a-cigarette in California.

14. Q's latest gadget only locates your car keys.

13. Just when you think you've finally found the right girl to settle down with, she tries to jam a pen into your throat.

12. His car may be a computerized, kick-ass arsenal, but try putting a Super Big Gulp in the cup holder.

11. Morons at Jiffy Lube always pouring windshield-washer fluid in the napalm tank.

10. Embarrassing to have girlfriend's name paged when separated at Wal-Mart.

9. If his neighbor pulls that "Finkelbaum. Morris Finkelbaum." crap one more time, he's getting an ice pick in the forehead.

8. New Bond girl RuPaul always kicking his ass at arm wrestling.

7. Studio budget cutbacks have him at the wheel of a souped-up 1976 Gremlin with new Bond girl, Bea Arthur.

6. Post–Cold War villains? Evil Dr. Hemorrhoid and the Tucks Twins.

5. Always looks like a ninny in Sean Connery's big-ass shoes.

4. Wet spot in bed usually contains bullet hole.

3. Picture on license to kill looks terrible.

2. Increasing competition for beautiful women spies from American agent Double-Chin Bubba.

1. Pussy Galore = herpes galore

The list on the preceding page is from January 13, 1998.
It was compiled from 152 submissions from 54 contributors.

Paul Paternoster, Redwood City, CA	– 1, 15
William Gray, San Jose, CA	– 2
Dan Signer, Studio City, CA	– 3
Bruce Ansley, Baltimore, MD	– 4
Don Swain, Pontiac, MI	– 5
Daniel Weckerly, Limerick, PA	– 6
Caroline Gennity, Virginia Beach, VA	– 7, 9
Jeff Downey, Raleigh, NC	– 7
Chuck Smith, Woodbridge, VA	– 8, 14
Chris White, New York, NY	– 8
John Voigt, Chicago, IL	– 10, 11
Jennifer Hart, Arlington, VA	– 12
R.M. Weiner, Somerville, MA	– 13
Dave Henry, Slidell, LA	– 16
Bob Mader, Knoxville, TN	– 17
Jeff Scherer, Brooklyn, NY	– 17
Kevin Freels, Sun Valley, CA	– Topic

The first thing you should do when
you get up is read the obituaries.
You never know when you'll see
a name that will just make your day.

(Ed Salisbury)

A wise man once told me,
"Violence is not the answer."
But if the question is, "How do I get wise
men to mind their own freaking business?"
then I think violence *is* the answer.

(Matt Diamond)

The Top 16 Olympic Events in Hell

16. Curling

15. Removing Plastic Clamp Sensor From Just-Purchased Clothing With Common Household Utensil Competition

14. Discus Inferno

13. 666-Yard Ass-Luge Down a Razor Blade Into Cold Alcohol

12. Naked Hot Oil Sumo Wrestling

11. Marge Schott-Put

10. Beelzebubsledding

9. Giant Slalom and Gomorrah

8. Synchronized Sinning

7. Men's 50000000000000000000-Meter Barefoot Speed Skating

6. Pummel Horse

5. Mobius Strip "Loogie" Luge

4. Karla Faye Tucker Pickaxe Toss

3. Disfigure Skating

2. Lawyer vs. Insurance Salesman Speed-Talking Competition

1. Clean 'n' Sober Snowboarding

The list on the preceding page is from February 12, 1998. It was compiled from 129 submissions from 46 contributors.

Jennifer Hart, Arlington, VA	– 1
Annie Fisher, Philadelphia, PA	– 2
Dave Wesley, Pleasant Hill, CA	– 3
Beth Kohl, Chicago, IL	– 4
Fred Hesby, Portland, OR	– 5, 12
David G. Scott, Kansas City, MO	– 5
Ed Smith, Chattanooga, TN	– 5
Daniel Weckerly, Limerick, PA	– 6
Bob Mader, Knoxville, TN	– 7
Keith Martin, Atlanta, GA	– 7
Larry Hollister, Concord, CA	– 8, 10
Denis Rubin, Los Angeles, CA	– 9, 14
Kevin Hawley, Fairless Hills, PA	– 10, 16
R.M. Weiner, Somerville, MA	– 10
Jim Rosenberg, Greensboro, NC	– 11
Caroline Gennity, Virginia Beach, VA	– 12
Chuck Smith, Woodbridge, VA	– 13
Mitch Patterson, Atlanta, GA	– 13
Jennifer Markes, West Hollywood, CA	– 15, Topic
Bruce Ansley, Baltimore, MD	– 16
Sam Evans, Charleston, SC	– 16
Dave Henry, Slidell, LA	– 16
Troy Roberson, Birmingham, AL	– 16
Jeff Scherer, Brooklyn, NY	– 16
Josh Fruhlinger, Oakland, CA	– 16

You can get a free meal at most seafood restaurants if you order lobster and, upon arrival of the meal, hysterically cry out, "This is the lobster that killed my parents!" This doesn't work as well with pizza though, so don't even bother.

(George MacMillan)

The Top 15 Movie Quotes We'd Like to See (Part I)

15. "Wait — why don't we look for a campground that isn't plagued by a homicidal maniac?"

14. "Oh, come on, Clarisse... just a nibble?"

13. "That's great, Will. Now solve *this* equation: How many times does a toilet have to back up before the whole damn math building stinks?"

12. "The truth? You can't handle the truth! You're a freakin' Scientologist!"

11. "Since the 10 of us are surrounding Mr. Van Damme, let's attack him one at a time. It just makes sense."

10. "Dad, can I borrow the Death Star tonight?"

9. "Okay, Jack, I will, but only because we're probably gonna be dead in an hour."

8. "He can't be bargained with. He can't be reasoned with. He doesn't feel fear, or pain, or remorse. And until he is found guilty of *something*, there's no stopping the Clintonator!"

7. "The name's Jeremy. Ron Jeremy."

6. "Mrs. Robinson, promise me you'll never discuss this with the independent counsel."

5. "You know, Sally, rather than waste that talent in a deli, why don't we open a phone-sex business?"

4. "I'm sorry, Dave, I can't do that without Microsoft PodBay 2.1."

3. "Wardrobe! See if you can find Ms. Stone some panties."

2. "Thelma, I think we missed our turn."

1. "This could be the beginning of a beautiful friendsh— Hey! Get your hand off my ass!!"

The list on the preceding page is from March 27, 1998.
It was compiled from 90 submissions from 34 contributors.

Lev L. Spiro, Los Angeles, CA	– 1
Gene Markins-Dieden, New Haven, CT	– 2
Sharon Silva, Clarksville, TN	– 3
Jonathan D. Colan, Miami, FL	– 4, 6
Dave Henry, Slidell, LA	– 5, 9, 14
John Voigt, Chicago, IL	– 7
Jeff Scherer, Brooklyn, NY	– 8
Peg Warner, Exeter, NH	– 10
LeMel Hebert-Williams, San Fran., CA	– 11
Bill Muse, Seattle, WA	– 12
Jim Rosenberg, Greensboro, NC	– 13
Mark Schmidt, Santa Cruz, CA	– 15
Chris White, New York, NY	– Topic

To demonstrate my superior intellect,
I have decided to join Menses.

(Jonathan Struhs)

A good book can transport you to faraway places.
Especially a really big book with wheels on
the bottom and a jet engine mounted on the back.

(Dave Lartigue)

I just can't read National Geographic any more.
I'm tired of being reminded that I suck
at carrying heavy things on my head.

(John Gephart)

The Top 15 Movie Quotes We'd Like to See (Part II)

15. "Go ahead, make my... man, this gun is heavy!"

14. "Man, that corpse in the front seat of my prop plane is *really* starting to reek."

13. "For the love of God, can't you people see it's not a woman but a man *dressed* as a woman?!"

12. "Well, my dear, let's just see if you give a damn when I hire the best divorce lawyer in Atlanta and take you for half of everything you've got!"

11. "All right, track down the prop master and get the Orgasmatron back on the set."

10. "I just felt a great disturbance in the Force... or maybe it was that pastrami sandwich."

9. "Frankly, my dear, I don't give a rat's ass."

8. "McClain! You know that building you destroyed? It's coming out of your paycheck!"

7. "If you build it, they will pay $45 for box seats."

6. "For cryin' out loud, Chewy, use the friggin' sandbox, willya?!"

5. "I'm sorry, Dirk, but I'm just not into long-distance relationships."

4. "Sorry, Captain, I thought there was a tribble on your head. I'll buy you a new one."

3. "Use the fork, Luke."

2. "No, monsieur, find something else — I need the butter for the quiche."

1. "Oh, my God! They killed Freddy! You bastards!"

The list on the preceding page is from March 30, 1998.
It was compiled from 131 submissions from 44 contributors.

Paul Schindler, Orinda, CA	– 1
Glenn Marcus, Washington, DC	– 2, 15
Perry Friedman, Menlo Park, CA	– 3
Jim Rosenberg, Greensboro, NC	– 4
Michelle Burke, San Francisco, CA	– 5
Rob Wells, Paris, France	– 6
Greg Sadosuk, Fairfax, VA	– 7
Eric Huret, Atlanta, GA	– 8
Larry Hollister, Concord, CA	– 9, 10
Jeff Scherer, Brooklyn, NY	– 9
Cathie Walker, Victoria, BC, Canada	– 9
Chuck Smith, Woodbridge, VA	– 11
Ed Smith, Chattanooga, TN	– 12
Tony Hill, Minneapolis, MN	– 13
Peter Rogers, Boston, MA	– 14
Chris White, New York, NY	– Topic

If I ever have a kid, I think it would
be cool to teach him some weird
code language only he and I know.
That way, he wouldn't be able to incriminate me
if they find him in the cage in the basement.

(Craig Stacey)

My girlfriend is more of a left outer join,
but I'm more of a right inner join kind of guy.
Sure, you may not think it's funny,
but if you'd ever used SQL Server, you'd
be soiling your pants laughing by now.

(Mark Niebuhr)

The Top 16 Rejected Motel 6 Slogans

16. We're working on that smell thing, too.

15. Because you deserve better than the back seat of some car.

14. As seen on *COPS*.

13. If we'd known you were staying all night, we'd have changed the sheets.

12. Not just for nooners anymore.

11. We left off the 9, but you know it's there.

10. You rented the room, now buy the video.

9. Sure, you could stay someplace nicer, but then you wouldn't have money left over for a hooker.

8. We'll leave the Lysol for ya!

7. Hey, we're not the Ritz, but just try banging your secretary there on *your* salary, pal!

6. We don't make the adultery. We make the adultery better.

5. It's hookerriffic!

4. Official lodging of the 1998 Florida Marlins.

3. Blurring the line between stains and avant-garde sheet art since 1962!

2. Cheap and easy — just like your mother.

1. We put the *ho* in *motel*.

The list on the preceding page is from April 10, 1998.
It was compiled from 152 submissions from 54 contributors.

Jim Rosenberg, Greensboro, NC	– 1, 6
Beth Kohl, Chicago, IL	– 2
Caroline Gennity, Virginia Beach, VA	– 3, 9
Don Swain, Pontiac, MI	– 4
Fred Hesby, Portland, OR	– 5
Christopher Troise, New York, NY	– 7
Larry Hollister, Concord, CA	– 8
Don Horton, Sacramento, CA	– 10
Gene Markins-Dieden, New Haven, CT	– 11
Bill Muse, Seattle, WA	– 12
Bruce Ansley, Baltimore, MD	– 13
John Voigt, Chicago, IL	– 14
Josh Fruhlinger, Oakland, CA	– 15
Greg Pettit, Houston, TX	– 15
Mark Schmidt, Santa Cruz, CA	– 16
Paul Paternoster, Redwood City, CA	– Topic

Everyone has a party trick. Mine is
to wait until everyone has passed out,
then go home with their wallets and
jewelry and the rest of the alcohol.

(Nerissa Rowan)

I think a good movie would be about a guy who
always gets up every morning to discover
another limb has grown from his body.
Man, I'd rent that three or four times.
But on the fourth time, I'd probably just
fast-forward to the part about the tongues.

(LeMel Hebert-Williams)

The Top 16 Hockey Player Pick-Up Lines

16. "What do you say we drop the gloves and go at it?"

15. "Look, my teeth spell out 'I love you' in block letters!"

14. "My other stick curves to the right."

13. "So this guy says he hates hockey players because they have no tact and are easily distracted, and I... Hey, babe, wanna screw?"

12. "Bagy, yrrr so beurdiffle dat I feel I can be nacheral wif yoo."

11. "You heard right: I only take off this mask for two things."

10. "I said, 'Would you like a *puck*?'"

9. "You know, fewer teeth means more tongue!"

8. "I may be toothless, sweaty and all black and blue, but I make a mean quiche Lorainne."

7. "I only drool when I'm standing upright."

6. "Hi, I'm Zam. How would you like a Zamboni ride?"

5. "Well if I can't score, can I get an assist?"

4. "Tho... what'th your thighn?"

3. "C'mon, baby, the iceman cometh... but never too soon."

2. "Me take you eat."

1. "We're gonna go beat up Scott Hamilton. Wanna come?"

The list on the preceding page is from May 13, 1998.
It was compiled from 132 submissions from 48 contributors.

Bill Muse, Seattle, WA	– 1
John Voigt, Chicago, IL	– 2
Lev L. Spiro, Los Angeles, CA	– 3
Peg Warner, Exeter, NH	– 4
Kevin Hawley, Fairless Hills, PA	– 5
Mark Schmidt, Santa Cruz, CA	– 6
Don Swain, Pontiac, MI	– 7
Peter Bauer, Rochester, NY	– 8
Greg Pettit, Houston, TX	– 9, 10
Greg Sadosuk, Fairfax, VA	– 11
Alexander Clemens, San Francisco, CA	– 12
David G. Scott, Kansas City, MO	– 13
Tom Louderback, Boston, MA	– 14
Phil Doyle, Mercer Island, WA	– 15
Jonathan D. Colan, Miami, FL	– 16
Chris White, New York, NY	– Topic

I don't see what the big deal
is about same-sex marriages.
Every married couple I know
has the same sex all the time.

(Jim Rosenberg)

It's just an old superstition that when
you snap someone's photo you steal their
soul. But there's no way I'm gonna tell
that to my grandmother. Not until I can
afford to hire a real maid, anyway.

(Andy Ihnatko)

The Top 14 Signs Your Online Relationship Isn't Working Out

14. You discover that Chesty McBust isn't her real name, and she's dialing in from Langley, Va.

13. You: large, hairy man
    Your online girlfriend: large, hairy man

12. Her postmaster rejects your e-mail not as "undeliverable" but as "unlikely to get you anywhere."

11. After months of shared experiences and emotional investments, she attacks you in the Mines of Quarn with a +5 Vorpal Sword when she learns you're worth 45,000 points.

10. "Returned mail: User unknown and never wants to hear from you again."

9. Your cyberlover is always busy editing that silly little Top 5 List.

8. Getting perhaps a bit too comfortable, she lets a reference to cutting her chin shaving slip by.

7. You discover that she's been cutting and pasting her orgasms.

6. You can barely make out her face in the JPEG she sent because she's obscured by her 25 cats.

5. He claims to be the richest man in the world, but his GIF looks like some geek who works for a software company.

4. Since her first e-mail, MakeMoneyFast!@cyber-promotions.com has become cold and distant.

3. She's suddenly changed her address to comingout@lesbian.com.

2. Ken Starr launches an investigation into your relationship with the mysterious tubby@whitehouse.gov.

1. In an ironic twist of fate, you discover that the object of your affection is a curvaceous 18-year-old rather than the geeky 14-year-old boy she'd pretended to be.

The list on the preceding page is from July 17, 1998.
It was compiled from 132 submissions from 47 contributors.

Don Swain, Pontiac, MI	– 1
Matt Chaput, Calgary, Alberta, Canada	– 2
Beth Kohl, Chicago, IL	– 3
Mark Schmidt, Santa Cruz, CA	– 3
Jon Litfin, Columbus, OH	– 4
Alexander Clemens, San Francisco, CA	– 5
Tisha Stacey, Lisle, IL	– 6
Keith Martin, Atlanta, GA	– 7
David W. James, Los Angeles, CA	– 8
Carla Brandon, San Diego, CA	– 9
Paul Paternoster, Redwood City, CA	– 10
Rob Seulowitz, New York, NY	– 11
Dave Wesley, Pleasant Hill, CA	– 12
David Bryant, Columbia, MD	– 13
Kim Moser, New York, NY	– 14
Bruce Ansley, Baltimore, MD	– Topic

If I were a dairy cow, I don't know
which I'd prefer — the leisurely life
of nonstop grazing or the daily sessions
with a machine massaging my nipples.

(Chris White)

Sometimes I wish human beings had the power
to regenerate lost appendages. But not if that
flab of skin that used to hang from my elbow
counts as an appendage. I couldn't bear to
think of having to sand *that* thing off again.

(J.P. Styskal)

The Top 12 Ways Life Would Be Different if There Were No Vowels

12. Wht th fck knd f tpc s ths?

11. Nothing before nothing except after *c*? Sure, Teach. Whatever.

10. Comic strip characters limited to sleeping and swearing.

9. Sudden inability to pick out the Czech hockey players in the NHL.

8. Alex Trebek: still wealthy and famous.
   Pat and Vanna: living in a van down by the river and fighting tooth and press-on nail over dwindling supply of food.

7. As the price of *Sesame Street* stock plummets, Bert and Ernie are laid off.

6. *Y*, during interrogation, denies ever working for the deposed junta.

5. Nineteen percent less time on the crapper.

4. The Thomas Brothers' Map company regional offices in Honolulu do some serious downsizing.

3. Now, *51* ways to leave your lover! Latest addition: "Sorry, babe, but *U* and *I* are history."

2. Old MacDonald awakens to an eerie silence.

1. President Clinton breathes a sigh of relief, since he never said he didn't have sex with Mnc Lwnsk.

The list on the preceding page is from July 30, 1998.
It was compiled from 119 submissions from 44 contributors.

Blair Bostick, Alexandria, VA	– 1, 7
Larry Hollister, Concord, CA	– 2, 3
Jonathan D. Colan, Miami, FL	– 2
Kevin Freels, Sun Valley, CA	– 4
Matt Loiselle, Detroit, MI	– 5
Alexander Clemens, San Francisco, CA	– 6, 8
Dave Henry, Slidell, LA	– 7
Whit Andrews, Omaha, NE	– 8, 11
Craig Stacey, Lisle, IL	– 9
Paul Seaburn, Houston, TX	– 10
Ed Smith, Chattanooga, TN	– 11
Geoff Brown, Farmington Hills, MI	– 12
Jim Rosenberg, Greensboro, NC	– 12
Marshal Perlman, Minneapolis, MN	– Topic

My boss caught me swigging whiskey
and chasing it with tequila shots.
Hey, I *told* him I was multi-flasking.

(J. Hutter)

That's the last time I'll ever steal
a plastic bag from someone walking a dog!

(Ken Prentice)

I think McDonald's should have a "McHooves"
meal. No sense letting that crap go to waste.

(Jim Rosenberg)

The Top 12 Signs Football Season Is Starting

12. *Jerry Springer* is no longer the only place to watch large asses crammed into tight shiny pants.

11. Ross Perot warns Americans about a giant sucking sound coming from the Louisiana Superdome.

10. Groundhog emerges, sees shadow, gets drunk and sexually assaults a passing gopher.

9. Mike Ditka's blood pressure can now be measured from the Hubble telescope using a simple infrared filter.

8. Al Michaels is seen beating his head against a tree stump to prepare for yet another mind-numbing season in the broadcast booth with Dan Dierdorf.

7. Foreplay now involves dressing provocatively as Arrowhead Stadium.

6. Word is out in Dallas: Even one snotty little Cowboy joke on the Top 5 List and Chris White's ass is grass.

5. Fistfights have moved from the Beanie Baby aisle to the creatine aisle.

4. National supply of "C" batteries depleted as football widows stock up for the season.

3. Ass-pattings up an astonishing 119 percent.

2. John Madden throws out the ceremonial first wildly cartoonish hyperbole and gesticulation.

1. It's okay to say the word "Packer" again within a group of guys.

The list on the preceding page is from September 8, 1998.
It was compiled from 87 submissions from 36 contributors.

Sam Evans, Charleston, SC	– 1
Martell Stroup, Boston, MA	– 2
Jim Rosenberg, Greensboro, NC	– 3, 9
Peter Rogers, Boston, MA	– 3
Fred Hesby, Portland, OR	– 4
Chuck Smith, Woodbridge, VA	– 4
Steve Hurd, San Ramon, CA	– 5
Ed Smith, Chattanooga, TN	– 6
David G. Scott, Kansas City, MO	– 7
Kevin Hawley, Fairless Hills, PA	– 8
Lev L. Spiro, Los Angeles, CA	– 10
Bill Muse, Seattle, WA	– 11
Larry Hollister, Concord, CA	– 12
Jonathan D. Colan, Miami, FL	– Topic

If I ever die by being buried alive
in something, I hope it's something
good, like boobs or chicken wings.

(Scott E. Frank)

If smoking is so bad, why is the first thing they
have you make in school art class an ashtray?

(Derek Winsworth)

"You can never be too rich or too thin."
I think that would make a great
tattoo for a lottery-winning anorexic.

(Jennifer Ritzinger)

Going on vacation is great.
First, you don't have to go to work,
and then if you're lucky, the people
at the airport strip-search you.

(Slick Sharkey)

I think if you really like a girl, you
have to pay a *lot* of attention to her.
But try telling that to those jerks on the jury.

(Dave George)

I can't decide between *Computers for Morons*
and *The Complete Idiot's Guide to Computers*.
Sometimes I wish such choices were simpler.

(Bob Van Voris)

I have always dreamed of writing and
seeing my work up on the big screen.
My dream finally came true when my
bowling team asked me to keep score.

(J. Hutter)

Well my neighbor's teenage daughter is off to
college next year, and you know what that means:
I'm going to have buy a much stronger telescope.

(Brent A. McDaniel)

A wise man once taught me
about the benefits of flatulence.
I'll never forget the years
I spent under his tutelage.

(Randy Saint)

You can lead a horse to water, but you can't
make him drink. Actually, this rule applies
to anyone whom you routinely humiliate with
saddles, riding whips and involuntary servitude.

(George MacMillan)

Every time I try to give blood, they won't accept it.
Maybe it's time I try giving my own blood.

(Paul Paternoster)

I got some bad news today.
You know the money you get
from those ATM machines?
It comes from *your* account!

(Jim Rosenberg)

If ignorance is bliss, then
I must be the happiest
thingamajigee in the whatchamacallit!

(R.M. Weiner)

The Top 13 Signs the Opposite Sex Is Repelled by You

13. Your bra strap is constantly getting snagged in your back hair.

12. British accent? Check.
    British sports car? Check.
    Austin Powers teeth? Uhh! Not groovy!

11. Dorky glasses? Check.
    Five-dollar hairdo? Check.
    Multi-billion-dollar software fortune? Uh-oh...

10. You think you look simply smashing in your tailor-made XXXXL Starfleet uniform.

9. Viagra has copyrighted your image, including it with each prescription as "the anti-coronary emergency antidote."

8. The last time anyone said "yes" to you, your question was, "You want fries with that?"

7. Your prom date was a sock puppet.

6. Even the ewes in the north forty have been acting stand-offish of late.

5. Men tell you they think of you during sex and that it works better than baseball scores.

4. Rather than spend two weeks with you in some hoity-toity East Coast resort town, your husband would rather get involved in a relationship that starts with a cigar and some oral sex and eventually progresses to missile attacks in two countries.

3. Always firing warning shots into your groin.

2. Didn't anyone ever explain that pus is *not* an acceptable substitute for KY Jelly?

1. No matter what *you* think, Chester, "front or back" makes a big difference to the old rolled-up-sock-in-the pants trick.

The list on the preceding page is from September 11, 1998.
It was compiled from 97 submissions from 37 contributors.

Kevin Hawley, Fairless Hills, PA	– 1, 12
Chuck Smith, Woodbridge, VA	– 2
Mark Weiss, Austin, TX	– 3
Dave Henry, Slidell, LA	– 4, 7
Michelle Burke, San Francisco, CA	– 4
Tony Hill, Minneapolis, MN	– 5
Lev L. Spiro, Los Angeles, CA	– 6
David G. Scott, Kansas City, MO	– 8
David W. James, Los Angeles, CA	– 9
Matt Siske, Dayton, OH	– 9
Greg Pettit, Houston, TX	– 10, 13
Peter Rogers, Boston, MA	– 11
LeMel Hebert-Williams, San Francisco, CA	– Topic

Who cares how many angels can
dance on the head of a pin?
I want to know how many can
mosh in the middle of a Froot Loop.

(Marko Peric)

Sometimes when I go for job interviews,
I get the feeling that they don't give enough
consideration to my Ph.D. in document forgery.

(Paul Hannah)

I wish I could talk to my doctor about erectile
dysfunction, but for some reason it never comes up.

(Scott E. Frank)

The Top 13 Ways the British Royal Family Can Modernize the Monarchy

13. Lop off Charlie's ears for streamlined aerodynamic styling and increased fuel-efficiency.

12. Trade in royal sceptre for a huge foam finger with "Born to Rule!" on it.

11. Group appearance on *Jerry Springer* on "Inbreeding Monarchies" week.

10. Get Spotted Dick off the royal menu once and for all.

9. Elton John tributes for everybody!

8. Convicted witches now microwaved at the stake.

7. Have the queen wear her tiara backward and rap her speeches as The Notorious H.R.M. Liz Crowny Crown and the RoyL Cru.

6. Upgrade royal boombox from 8-track to cassette.

5. www.ourfirstbeheading.com

4. Void left by Ginger filled by the Queen Mum as "Dustfarter Spice."

3. For knighthood ceremony: Out with the sword, in with the head butt!

2. Replace wooden stick up ass with graphite stick up ass.

1. Two words: extreme foxhunting

The list on the preceding page is from October 1, 1998. It was compiled from 121 submissions from 43 contributors.

Larry Hollister, Concord, CA	– 1
David Hyatt, New York, NY	– 2
Martell Stroup, Boston, MA	– 2
Jason Anderson, Birmingham, AL	– 3
Kevin Hawley, Fairless Hills, PA	– 4
Patrick Douglas Crispen, U of AL	– 5
Rich Taylor, Arlington, VA	– 6
Lisa Oliver, London, England	– 7, 12, Topic
Bill Muse, Seattle, WA	– 7, 13
Jason Anthoine, Alpharetta, GA	– 7
Tim McKemy, Chandler, AZ	– 8
Peter Rogers, Boston, MA	– 9
Chuck Smith, Woodbridge, VA	– 10
Mitch Patterson, Atlanta, GA	– 11

You know how everyone laughs when one of your friends makes you promise to shoot her in the head if you ever catch her doing the the Electric Slide? Turns out she was just kidding.

(Will Middelaer)

First I thought the monkey I bought was cool, then I thought all the springs I bought were even cooler, then I thought the hundreds of mirrors I bought were the coolest — but all in all, I learned that a springing monkey gets freaked out by all those friggin' mirrors.

(Mark Niebuhr)

The Top 14 Sports Phrases Used During the Sex Championships

14. It's gonna take a minute for him to reload the chamber.

13. He's bound to land in the penalty box for hooking.

12. She's going for a new record in the clean and jerk.

11. Looks like he's been spending too much time "choking the coach."

10. He appeared to come out of nowhere.

9. And there's the two-minute warning!

8. Now he's got three balls on him.

7. Ooh... that's gonna leave a mark!

6. Now they're gonna go man-to-man.

5. Time out while he dons the protective gear.

4. Unbelievable! Cox has gone to the mound 11 times tonight! That's gotta be a record!

3. Looks like he's a couple of inches short.

2. They're bringing out the chains.

1. GOOOOOOOOAAAAAAAALLLLLLLLLL!!!
   GOOOOOOOOAAAAAAAALLLLLLLLLL!!!
   GOOOOOOOOAAAAAAAALLLLLLLLLL!!!

The list on the preceding page is from October 7, 1998. It was compiled from 129 submissions from 41 contributors.

Paul Paternoster, Los Altos Hills, CA	– 1, Topic
Tom Louderback, Boston, MA	– 1
Marshal Perlman, Minneapolis, MN	– 1
Mark Weiss, Austin, TX	– 1
Ken Woo, Encinitas, CA	– 1
Kevin Hawley, Fairless Hills, PA	– 1
David Hyatt, New York, NY	– 2
John Hering, Alexandria, VA	– 3, 8
Sue Prifogle Otte, Rushville, IN	– 4
Ann Bartow, Dayton, OH	– 5
Lev L. Spiro, Los Angeles, CA	– 6
Paul Schindler, Orinda, CA	– 7
Larry Hollister, Concord, CA	– 9
Michael Wolf, Brookline, MA	– 9
Lisa Oliver, London, England	– 10
Michelle Burke, San Francisco, CA	– 11
David G. Scott, Kansas City, MO	– 12
Peter Rogers, Boston, MA	– 13
Matt Loiselle, Detroit, MI	– 14

I tried to get in touch with my "inner child" once. Now I have to register with the local police every time I change my mind.

(Kevin Browne)

If I ever won the lottery, I'd probably buy a tank and just spend my days running over stuff.

(John Gephart)

The Top 15 Worst Blues Singer Names

15. Willie "White Shoes After Labor Day" Lumpkin

14. Charlie "Sittin' in First Class and Cheerful as Hell" Pickett

13. Al "Lightnin'" Gore

12. The Suspiciously Clean-Shaven, Well-Coiffed Artist in the Dark Glasses Who Won't Admit That He Was Formerly Known as John Tesh and Is Now Playing Barrelhouse Boogie-Woogie to Earn a Buck

11. John Lee Crackwhore

10. Timmy "Up With People" Perkyman

9. Tie: "Portly Dan" Aykroyd and Bruce "Shinehead" Willis

8. Matt "Sleeping With Cameron Diaz" Dillon

7. Winston P. "Sunshine Man" Walthrop III, King of the Cape Cod Blues

6. Tiny Red Johnson

5. Screamin' Josh Rabinowitz

4. Mack "Crusty Underthings" Morton

3. Stanley "Stank Ass" Wilson

2. Bawlin' Wimp

1. Luther "Kill Me, Just Kill Me" Johnson

The list on the preceding page is from October 8, 1998.
It was compiled from 183 submissions from 64 contributors.

Kevin Freels, Burbank, CA	– 1
Jim Rosenberg, Greensboro, NC	– 2
Kevin Hawley, Fairless Hills, PA	– 3
David W. James, Los Angeles, CA	– 4
Lev L. Spiro, Los Angeles, CA	– 5
M.J. Finan, Cleveland, OH	– 6
Peter Bauer, Rochester, NY	– 7
Matt Chaput, Calgary, Alberta, Canada	– 7
Tony Hill, Minneapolis, MN	– 7
Gene Markins-Dieden, New Haven, CT	– 8
Peter Rogers, Boston, MA	– 9
Brian Jones, Atlanta, GA	– 9
Martell Stroup, Boston, MA	– 10
Jeff Scherer, Brooklyn, NY	– 11
Tom Bestor, Oakland, CA	– 11
John Treusch, Burlington, NJ	– 12
Jeff Downey, Raleigh, NC	– 13
Marshal Perlman, Minneapolis, MN	– 14
Geoff Brown, Farmington Hills, MI	– 14
Jason Anderson, Birmingham, AL	– 15
Tom Louderback, Boston, MA	– Topic

I like to buy women a lot of drinks,
not so much to lessen their inhibitions
as to lower their standards.

(Damon Milhem)

I want my tombstone to read:
"We can't seem to find his body,"
because then maybe I'll still be alive.

(Slick Sharkey)

The Top 12 Ways to Annoy a Trekkie

12. Paint his Spock ears red for that "embarrassed Vulcan" look.

11. Interrupt James Doohan's convention speech by shouting, "Beam me up, Tubby!"

10. Tell her you've seen butthair more realistic than Kirk's toupee.

9. Tell him that it sounds like his Geo Metro's antimatter injection tubes are out of phase balance with the warp coils, then watch him go nuts trying to run a level-one diagnostic.

8. Wear the Starfleet badge upside down and loudly proclaim, "I am the Anti-Kirk!"

7. Point out that asking a woman if she fancies a Romulan ale whilst wearing your Klingon head prosthetic and ill-fitting Federation uniform is a terrible way to pull chicks.

6. Ask him why the phrase "gettin' to third base" is curiously absent from his Klingon glossary.

5. Tell him that in a parallel universe, women don't get nauseous at the sight of him.

4. Constantly remark that the relationship between Spock and Kirk has definite homosexual overtones.

3. Say, "Captain, I'm sensing a profound feeling of... geekiness."

2. Haul him into to court and threaten to end his virtual monopoly on PC operating systems.

1. When she asks if you'd like fries with that, reply, "Make it so, ho!"

The list on the preceding page is from October 28, 1998.
It was compiled from 116 submissions from 44 contributors.

Yoram Puius, Bronx, NY	– 1, 3, 6
Lloyd Jacobson, Washington, DC	– 2
Patrick Major, Dallas, OR	– 4
Bill Muse, Seattle, WA	– 4
JB Leibovitch, Oakland, CA	– 5
Gregory Swarthout, Murray, UT	– 5
Lisa Oliver, London, England	– 7
Shari Fisch, Jerusalem, Israel	– 8
Jonathan D. Colan, Miami, FL	– 9
Mark Weiss, Austin, TX	– 10
Greg Sadosuk, Fairfax, VA	– 11
Jennifer Ford, Fort Wayne, IN	– 12
Paul Paternoster, Los Altos Hills, CA	– Topic

I think it was pretty smart for them to freeze
Han Solo in carbonite. Had they chosen toffee,
he could've easily chewed his way to freedom.

(Brian Auten)

The biggest problem with being
the inventor of the time machine is that people
keep going back and stealing my idea.

(Ethan James)

I don't mind taking a risk as long as
I know everything will turn out okay.

(Barbara Rush)

The Top 13 Little-Known Phobias

13. "Hey, this is a nude beach! I ain't getting in that cold water!"
    Shrinkaphobia

12. "Get that #$%#-ing vodka bottle away from me!"
    Carmenelectraphobia

11. "He's coming straight for us — with his left turn signal on!"
    Oldfartophobia

10. "You have to push 'Start' to turn the damn computer off?!"
    Windophobia

9. "I won't go to your frat house to eat gyros and watch a tape of the Israel Philharmonic Orchestra on your old Sony VCR!"
   ThetaFetaMehtaBetaphobia

8. "Tonight on Paramount: 'Quickly, Gabrielle! We m—'" [CLICK]
   Xenaphobia

7. "*No*! Don't call the plumber!"
   Buttcrackophobia

6. "I don't want to watch *Friends*. The blonde chick freaks me out."
   Phoebephobia

5. "Um, doctor, why are you putting on that rubber glove?"
   Probeophobia

4. "You're busy Saturday? Well, how about next weekend then?"
   Rentanotherpornophobia

3. "It's *not* my imagination! Senator Helms is looking at me *that* way again!"
   Homophobophobia

2. "Wait! If we impeach him, then the new president will be...."
   aGoreophobia

1. "Honey, I bought a Corvette!"
   Smallpeniphobia

The list on the preceding page is from November 30, 1998. It was compiled from 91 submissions from 34 contributors.

Lev L. Spiro, Los Angeles, CA	– 1
Perry Friedman, Menlo Park, CA	– 2
Jim Rosenberg, Greensboro, NC	– 2
Larry Hollister, Concord, CA	– 2
Kate McClare, Ft. Lauderdale, FL	– 3, 8
Jonathan D. Colan, Miami, FL	– 4
Chuck Smith, Woodbridge, VA	– 5
Bill Muse, Seattle, WA	– 6
Rick Welshans, Alexandria, VA	– 7
Ann Bartow, Dayton, OH	– 8
John Hering, Alexandria, VA	– 8
Beth Kohl, Chicago, IL	– 8
Bruce Ansley, Baltimore, MD	– 9
Paul Schindler, Orinda, CA	– 10, 11
Kim Moser, New York, NY	– 10
Natasha Filipovic, New York, NY	– 12
Paul Paternoster, Los Altos Hills, CA	– 13
Mark Schmidt, Santa Cruz, CA	– Topic

When you *do* give a rat's ass,
nobody really appreciates that either.

(Elliott Downing)

If I had four arms, I'd probably be
a kick-ass juggler. Except that I'm not
too keen on that whole "practice" thing,
so I'd probably just use those extra arms
to scratch myself and hold more snacks.

(John Gephart)

The Top 15 Christian Coalition-Approved Nicknames for Breasts

15. Democrat Catchers

14. NFRU (Not for Recreational Use)

13. Pastor Baiters

12. Mounds of Shame

11. Heavenly Canteens

10. Pearly Weights

9. Hooteronomies

8. Pizza Pizza

7. Sweater Undulations

6. The Daughters of Lactiticus

5. Racks of Lambs of God

4. Communion Woofers

3. First and Second Mammalonians

2. Pamela 36:D

1. Beelzeboobs

The list on the preceding page is from December 15, 1998. It was compiled from 164 submissions from 59 contributors.

Kevin Hawley, Fairless Hills, PA	– 1
Michael Wolf, Brookline, MA	– 1
Yoram Puius, Bronx, NY	– 2
Peter Rogers, Boston, MA	– 2
Greg Sadosuk, Fairfax, VA	– 3
Doug Johnson, Santa Cruz, CA	– 4
Bill Muse, Seattle, WA	– 5
Daniel Weckerly, Limerick, PA	– 6
Jason Anderson, Birmingham, AL	– 7
Mark Weiss, Austin, TX	– 8
Jim Rosenberg, Greensboro, NC	– 9
Kevin Freels, Burbank, CA	– 10
John Voigt, Chicago, IL	– 11
Carla Brandon, San Diego, CA	– 12
Mitch Patterson, Atlanta, GA	– 13
Dave Henry, Slidell, LA	– 14
Lev L. Spiro, Los Angeles, CA	– 15
Sam Evans, Charleston, SC	– Topic

If I were ever in one of those jokes where you have to tell the native chief which way you'd prefer to die, I'd tell him that I'd like to be hung like a horse.

(Mike Cunningham)

When I asked my doctor why it hurt when I urinated, he pointed out that my penis was on fire. I guess that's why he's the doctor.

(Kevin Bonnay)

That's all, folks!

For more of the same, visit:

www.TopFive.com
www.Ruminate.com

Need more copies?

Take a good look at this fine publication, my friend. Note the care and craft with which it was assembled. Observe the loving manner in which the lists and Ruminations were meticulously prepared. Now ask yourself this one simple question:

"Wouldn't *The TopFive Guide to Fighting Evildoers* make a splendid gift for my family members, friends and co-workers, leading them to think I'm a generous person with exquisite taste and making them love me that much more?"

If you answered "yes," you should immediately make a copy of this page (or rip it right out of the book if you must) and use it to place an order for more copies. Remember: With so many evildoers in the world, society is counting on each of us do his or her part!

☐ Charge my credit card:
☐ VISA ☐ Mastercard ☐ American Express
Card # _____-_____-_____-_____ (Exp:___/___)

☐ Check or money order made out to TopFive.com enclosed.

Name: _____
Address: _____
City: _____ State/Province: _____
Zip/Postal Code: _____ Country: _____
E-mail Address: _____

Each book is $13.95. Add $3.50 total shipping for any number of books ordered. California residents add 8¼ % sales tax.

☐ Throw in a 1-year subscription to ClubTop5, TopFive's deluxe e-mail newsletter. Only $15 for a new list every weekday!

Mail this form with payment to: TopFive Publications
                                    5482 Wilshire Blvd., Suite 137
                                    Los Angeles, CA 90036

Or order online at our Web site: http://www.TopFive.com